FL

D1346340

75000012126 X

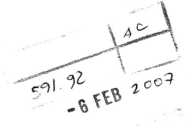

UNDERWATER CARIBBEAN

KURT AMSLER

WHITE STAR
PUBLISHERS

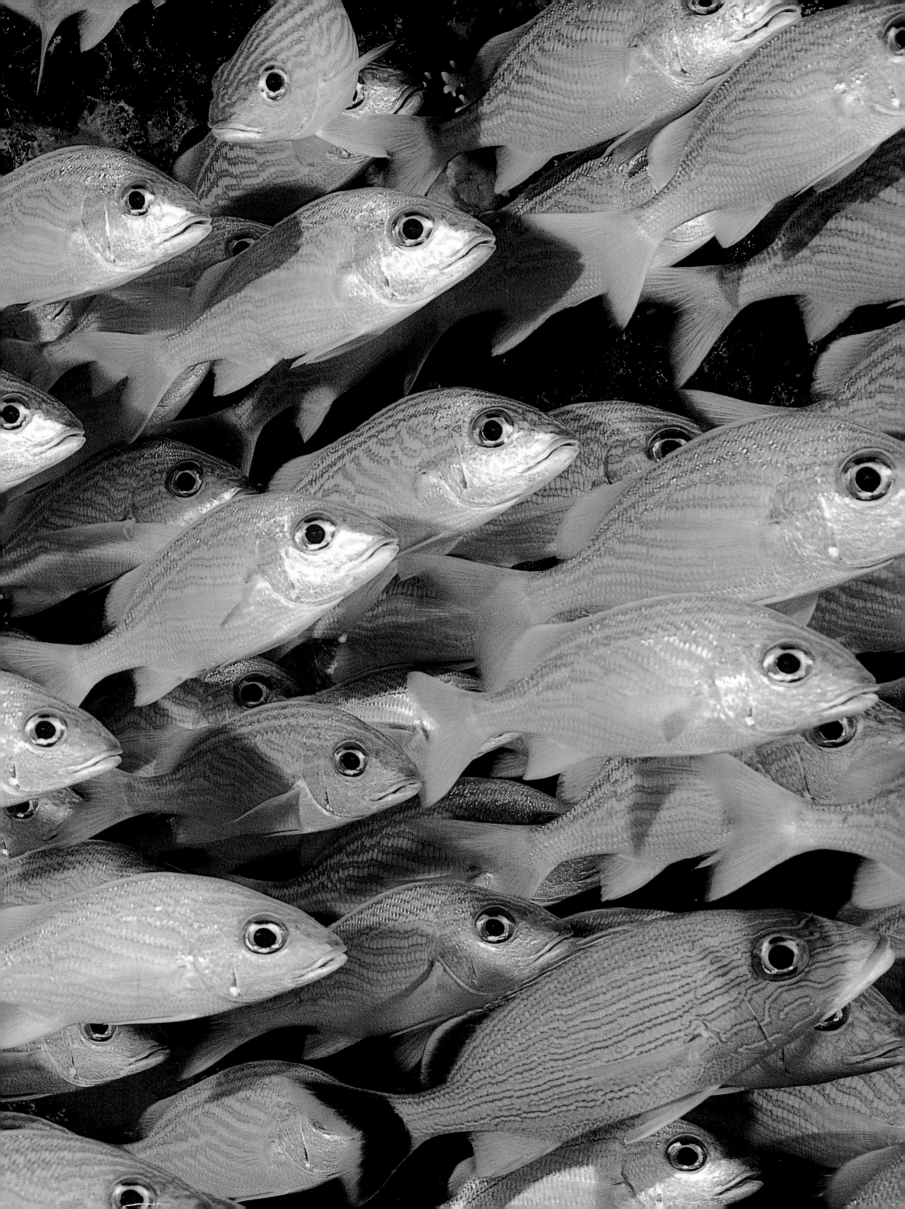

UNDERWATER CARIBBEAN

Texts and photographs
Kurt Amsler

Editors
Valeria Manferto De Fabianis
Laura Accomazzo

Scientific advice
Angelo Mojetta

Map
Cristina Franco

Graphic design
Anna Galliani

Translation
A.B.A. Srl, Milan

*The author would like to thank:
his wife Isabelle Amsler, Christopher J. Allison,
Aqua Safari, Renate Bernd, Joe M. Clark, John
Englander, Chris Ery, Cathy Church, Rebecca
Fitzgerald, Roger Fivat, Stephen Frink, crew of
Seafever, Maurits Groen, Doris Hagenbucher,
Bill Horn, Jacques Imbert, Ocean Touren,
Ocean Divers, Ben Rose, marco Rosenfelder, Ron
Reed, Crew of Rembrandt van Rijn, Kenneth
G. Thompson, Divemaster Kevin, Charles
Novalez, Unexso, Capt. Wesley, Frank Wirth.*

© 2004 White Star S.r.l.
Via Candido Sassone, 22-24
13100 Vercelli, Italy.
www.whitestar.it

ISBN: 88-544-0013-0

Reprints:
1 2 3 4 5 6 08 07 06 05 04

Printed in Singapour

CONTENTS

INTRODUCTION ..... page 14
A WORLD OF RARE BEAUTY ..... page 22
DOLPHINS: AMBASSADORS OF THE OCEAN ..... page 74
ANGELS OF THE SEA ..... page 82
THE SIRENS OF CHRISTOPHER COLUMBUS ..... page 92
NIGHT IN THE REEF ..... page 98
SPONGES: PLANTS OR ANIMALS? ..... page 124
STINGRAY CITY ..... page 136
THE WRECK OF SAINT-PIERRE ..... page 144
BLUE HOLE: A DIVE INTO THE STONEAGE ..... page 156

1 The great tubesponge, which can grow up to 2 metres tall, is one of the symbols of the Caribbean. Looking at these weird shapes, it isn't surprising that sponges were considered to be plants until the mid-19th century.

2-3 Halfmoon Cay, an island off Lighthouse Reef in Belize, resembles thousands of other West Indian islands: a stretch of sand covered with palm trees, bounded by a lagoon and the coral reef which plunges down into the ocean. In the background, a wreck which ran aground on the reef can be seen.

4-5 A large shoal of French grunts (*Haemulon flavolineatum*) has taken shelter near a coral wall. Their yellow-gold colour and the pale blue diagonal stripes on their backs make these fish one of the prettiest inhabitants of the reef.

6-7 The queen angelfish (*Holacanthus ciliaris*) certainly live up to their name. They swim around this underwater world with grace and elegance, as if aware of their beauty. The great sponges that can be seen in the image constitute the angelfish's favourite food.

8 The bluestriped grunt (*Haemulon sciurus*) is only encountered in shoals. The reason is simple: a group gives greater protection against enemies.

9 No other ocean in the world is so rich in soft coral and sponges in the surface waters as the Caribbean Sea. Corals and sponges are living creatures, not mere plants. These weird shapes, with their magnificent colours, consist of millions of tiny animals.

10-11 This Caribbean reefshark (*Carcharhinus perezi*) is 2 metres long. Much has been written about the danger of sharks, and this has given them a bad reputation; in reality they follow their instinct and aggression towards man is almost always caused by imprudence.

12-13 A shoal of southern stingray (*Dasyatis americana*) scours the sea bed in search of food, preferably prawns and other animals that live on the ocean floor.

INTRODUCTION

This part of the world has always held great interest, as demonstrated by its particularly eventful history. Today, this area to the west of the Atlantic Ocean is one of the most popular resorts with tourists from all over the world, attracted by the beauty of the subtropical archipelago. The sight which meets the tourist's eyes is a multitude of fairytale islands surrounded by turquoise water; an exotic landscape which changes dramatically from north to south, with a pleasantly mild climate. Divers who have the opportunity to explore here will be enchanted by the magical underwater world. The character of the inhabitants, with their infectious gaiety and their music, sets the scene. This corner of the Atlantic, which stretches between 110° and 180° longitude west and 30° and 10° latitude north, is usually called the Caribbean. This term was coined by the European conquerors; it derives from the name of the natives, called the Caribs. Nearly all the islands claim to have been visited by Christopher Columbus, as this represents a great tourist attraction, and call themselves Caribbean islands regardless of their position. However, the geographical borders are clearly defined. The true Caribbean Sea stretches between Cuba in the North, the Antilles in the East, Colombia and Venezuela in the South, and Central America (specifically Belize, Honduras and Nicaragua) in the West. North of the crescent-shaped island of Cuba in the Caribbean Sea and the Yucatan peninsula is the Gulf of Mexico, with the Bahamas Islands to the north-east. Sub-tropical flora and fauna are found in this arc both on land and under water because of the warm ocean currents. It all begins with the Equatorial Current which precedes the trade winds, moving west, pushing a huge mass of water against the islands. Part of the water is diverted north by the Bahamas, but most of it is channelled between Cuba and the Central American coast. Because of the obstacle represented by this stretch of land and the Gulf of Mexico the warm current suddenly changes direction; it moves east and then flows into the Atlantic as the Gulf Stream, which passes between Cuba and Florida.

The Caribbean contains some 7000 islands, which mainly differ in terms of size, type of vegetation, and above all the conformation of the land.

15 A French angelfish (*Pomacanthus paru*) in all its beauty. Divers and snorkellers can encounter the angels of the deep from the Florida Keys to the Antilles, from Venezuela to the Bermudas.

16 A grey angelfish (*Pomacanthus arcuatus*) hovers over a huge orange elephant-ear sponge. It doesn't seem to have decided whether to pay most attention to the photographer or to the diver swimming near the edge of the reef.

18-19 The diver seems to be swimming through a fairytale forest. Soft corals, sea plumes, sponges, hard corals and fire coral can be observed along the edge of the reef.

20-21 Horse-eye jacks (*Caranx latus*) are pelagic fish, which swim in large shoals along the reef. They normally hunt their prey in the open sea, though it is not unusual to see them darting in and out of the coral at incredible speed in search of a tasty morsel.

The Greater Antilles, comprising Cuba, Jamaica and the island of Hispaniola, which is divided between Haiti and the Dominican Republic, constitute the first group. The Lesser Antilles situated further south, which represent the second group, are classed on the basis of principles of navigation. They are divided between the Windward and Leeward Islands. The Leeward Islands, which lie further north, comprise the Virgin Islands, Anguilla, St. Maarten, Barbuda, Antigua, Montserrat and Guadeloupe. The Windward Islands extend from Dominica to Grenada and comprise Martinique, St. Lucia, St. Vincent and Barbados. To the north lie the Bahamas, and some 1000 kilometres further east in the Atlantic are the Bermuda Islands , which also benefit from the sub-tropical climate produced by the Gulf Stream. All these islands are surprising for the variety of their shapes. Some are almost round, others elongated, and others again extend like crescents across the dark blue sea. The Greater Antilles feature numerous mountains, contrasting dramatically with the Bahamas, which are entirely flat or feature fairly low hills. Pico Duarte, the highest peak in the Dominican Republic, reaches the respectable height of 3089 metres. These islands originated in two different periods. 70 million years ago, two branches were created by the extension of the mountain chains of Mexico and Central America. On one was present-day Jamaica, and on the other, the island of Cuba. The two islands are separated by an oceanic trench over 7000 metres deep. Primordial movements in the earth's crust, which led to the formation of mountain chains like the Rocky Mountains and the Andes in a later epoch, also affected the Caribbean, giving rise to hills and valleys.

Thus the southern islands became higher than the northern islands. The Windward Islands are nearly all of volcanic origin. They have a very varied landscape with numerous hills and volcanoes, some of which are still active. Although the volcanoes no longer represent a danger because of the installation of modern monitoring systems, the eruptions which occurred in the 19th and early 20th centuries killed thousands of people. The worst catastrophe was the eruption of the Montagne Pelée (Bare Mountain) on the French island of Martinique. After several days of unmistakeable warning signs, totally ignored by the authorities, on 8th May 1902 the mountain vomited a huge quantity of white-hot ash. The capital, Saint-Pierre, was destroyed in just a few minutes, and all its 30,000 inhabitants perished.

A WORLD OF RARE BEAUTY

Only a few parts of the world have such an eventful yet inglorious history as the Caribbean. Even before Christopher Columbus set foot on one of the present Bahamas Islands in 1492, on his first voyage, the islands were inhabited as far as the southern part. The Ciboney Indians, probably originating from Florida or South America, were the oldest inhabitants. Traces of them can be found in Cuba, Jamaica and Haiti. The Arawaks or Tainos, another Indian population of the Caribbean islands, originated from South America. Their culture was highly developed, and far surpassed that of the simpler Ciboneys. The Arawaks inhabited a very large area, as they undertook long and perilous voyages in their boats, which could carry up to 70 people. The peaceful existence of the Arawaks was rudely interrupted by the immigration of the Caribs from Brazil. This warlike population migrated from Venezuela and Honduras to the Lesser Antilles, taking the Arawaks by surprise with their fast ships and poison-tipped arrows. These well-organised warriors would no doubt have managed to conquer other islands too, if the Spanish conquistadors had not violently put an end to the long and glorious rule of the local inhabitants. In 1492 the dream of a lifetime came true for Christopher Columbus. On 3rd August he set sail with three caravels, the *Niña*, the *Pinta* and the *Santa Maria*, and headed west along an unknown route bound for the continent of Asia. The journey into the unknown lasted for weeks. Finally, on 12th October, land was sighted. They had reached one of the Bahamas Islands, which Columbus named San Salvador, from the name of the Saint Saviour. During the four voyages which took him further and further south, Columbus wrote extensively. There are also some letters to his sister and ship's logs in which he describes these lands in a romantic vein. In his descriptions of the Antilles, for example, he writes: "The air is perfumed, the trees are marvellous, and there are numerous springs of crystal-clear water. The natives have magnificent bodies, are polite and highly intelligent. The fish have uncommon colours, and a special kind of flower grows on the sea bed." In the pages about Cuba he claims never to have seen such a beautiful country, and tells of trees with huge leaves that were used as roofs for the houses. He also said the beach was studded with shells resembling mother-of-pearl, the water was of unparalleled clarity, and birdsong could be heard everywhere. The discovery of the New World might have had a different outcome if Christopher Columbus and his successors had devoted more time to nature study.

22-23 Coral reefs are made by living creatures. On a shelf formed by landslips, colonies consisting of billions of tiny animals have constructed a reef that reaches the surface. These creatures, called coral-building polyps, feed on the plankton in the water and secrete the calcareous substance of which coral is made.

23 bottom At the points where the reef reaches the surface, veritable islands have formed; some grow to reach considerable dimensions, while others have been transformed into the typical "Cays" of the Caribbean.

However, they all proved to have a single goal – to find gold and spices and exploit the land and its inhabitants. A highly significant comment in Columbus' log makes the aims of the conquistadors quite clear: "May it be God's will that I find good seams of gold today!". The discovery and conquest of much of the Caribbean towards the end of the 15th century is attributable to the Spaniards. Soon, however, these successes attracted the attention of other European powers to the new lands. In the early 16th century England and France, followed by the Netherlands, came into open conflict with Spain. The brutal corsairs at the service of the great powers also represented a constant threat to Spanish ships and their bases. Equally dangerous were incursions by pirates, who took orders from no-one and grew rich on the treasure they stole. This state of war continued until 1697, when Spain, England, the Netherlands and France signed the Treaty of Rijswijk. Part of the New World was allocated to each country, and from that time onwards, each power was free to exploit the new situation to the full. The way in which the colonial powers conquered these lands and subjugated the local populations is one of the most tragic episodes in recent history. This exploitation, and especially the martyrdom of the Indians, was openly condemned by a priest of French-Spanish descent called Bartolomé de las Casas. He managed to get two laws passed to improve the living conditions of the natives. However, in all good faith the priest advised the authorities to replace the Indians, who were threatened with extermination, with black workers imported from Africa, as he considered that they were stronger and better suited to the arduous work in the mines and fields. This rash advice led the Spaniards and other European countries to start importing manpower from Africa, and the slave trade became a significant economic factor which enabled the Spanish, Portuguese, English and French to grow rich. The countries from which slaves were imported were mainly located along the west coast of Africa, from Mauritania to Angola, as transport on the ships crammed with hundreds of chained negroes was simplest and cheapest from there. The slave trade, which was to last nearly two centuries, directly caused the death of tens of millions of Africans. Even the Church washed its hands of the tragedy of the black population, because most priests and representatives of the church had slaves at their service. Slavery, followed by its abolition and the freeing of the slaves, led to an unprecedented merging of races, and it is this unique mixture of populations and cultures which gives the Caribbean its special appeal.

24-25 The Belize barrier reef is the second-largest in the world. This huge coral belt runs from the Yucatan peninsula to beyond Honduras.

24 bottom Sights of this kind will delight even the most demanding diver. The bed of the lagoon can be seen through the crystal-clear water, and the point where the reef drops down to the ocean floor can be precisely identified.

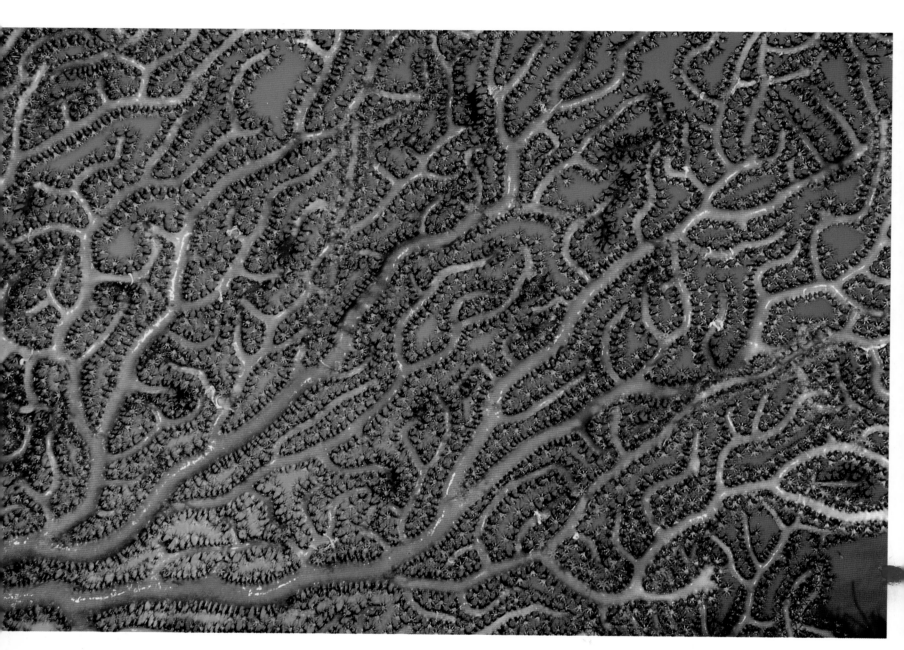

28 The deepwater sea fan *(Iciligorgia schrammi)* belongs to the gorgonian family. This close-up shows the tiny tentacles of the anthozoa, which capture the plankton in the water.

29 The deepwater sea fan *(Iciligorgia schrammi)* and various species of sponge cover a small bank of coral, as if an artist had painted an abstract picture using the brightest possible colours.

30-31 Unlike the impressive hard coral formations, these sea fans and sea plumes have an elastic structure. Apart from sponges, with their wide variety of shapes and colours, these filigree-work creatures are the most characteristic feature of the underwater world of the Caribbean.

32 This great star coral (*Montastrea cavernosa*) rises to the surface like a pillar. Every tiny crevice conceals a coral-building polyp; when darkness falls, they stretch out their tentacles to procure their food.

33 left This photo shows a branch of the slimy sea plume variety (*Pseudopterogorgia sp.*), which grows towards the sea surface. This kind of sea plumes grow in great bushes to as much as 2 metres tall.

33 right This porous sea rod (*Pseudoplexaura sp.*) is symmetrical. As in the case of most soft corals, the polyps are also active during the day, when they stretch their tentacles out of their pores.

The Caribbean Sea is not a coral sea like the Indian Ocean or the Pacific. Although the temperature of the water never falls below 20°C, in this case there is no true coral reef or even atolls, as reef-forming coral is absent. The ocean floor, made of limestone or lava rock, presents a fantastic interplay of overhanging rocks and caves, on which hard and soft corals were deposited at a later period. This layer was formed between and after the various Ice Ages.

At that time the sea level was much lower than it is now; environmental influences such as huge rivers, dramatic earth movements and violent volcanic eruptions gave the ocean floor its present conformation.

Divers entering one of the numerous caves in this area, whose entrances are now submerged, will discover stalactites and stalagmites in the great vaults; this demonstrates that the caves were dry in the past.

Sponges, with their countless shapes and colours, are typical of the underwater world of the Caribbean. Divers can find them at any depth; they are often so large that they can contain a man. There is also a huge amount of soft corals and sea fans. Some closely resemble the gorgonians of the Mediterranean, but most are endemic,

which means that they only live in these waters. Surprisingly, unlike those of other seas, the corals do not only live in the deepest areas, but can also be found immediately below the surface. Divers who swim over this mass of soft coral, rippling in the undertow, find themselves in a fairytale forest. In the shallower areas the hard corals form veritable reefs consisting of the menacing elkhorn coral, staghorn coral, yellow fire coral, slab coral and brain coral. The most spectacular feature of the underwater landscape in the Caribbean is represented by the precipices known as "drop-offs". Here, where the sea bed descends vertically for over 2000 metres to the continental shelf, a marvellous underwater world opens up for divers. The variety of life forms starts with the lower species, including snails, shells and worms with weird shapes, also found in other oceans. Crustaceans, including prawns, shrimps, crayfish and lobsters, scuttle along the reef.

34 This splendid, huge specimen of the common sea fan (*Gorgonia ventalina*) has been equipped by Nature with strong branches that taper towards the end to ensure greater flexibility, so that they can withstand even the strongest currents.

35 A diver's torch enlights the particular shape of a raw pore rope sponge (*Aplysina cauliformis*). This kind of sponges grow along the walls and can be found up to a depth of 150 metres.

Wherever you look, the most striking feature is the colour produced by thousands of little fish, so variegated that they look like the work of a mad artist. Some typical inhabitants of these waters are the huge angelfish, which can grow up to 40 centimetres long, being larger than the angelfish found in other seas.

Divers may come across the grey angelfish, the French angelfish, and the splendid queen angelfish with its brilliant yellow-blue colour. Only in these waters will divers and snorkellers encounter the striped Nassau grouper.

This fish grows to an impressive weight, and can be found in the places most popular with divers; these groupers are as docile as puppies, and are ready to follow visitors wherever they go. The shallow sand areas and the lagoons constitute the ideal habitat for some strange inhabitants of the sea bed.

They include the flat-bodied plaice, which in the course of its evolution has changed

36 This harmless-looking trumpetfish *(Aulostomus maculatus)*, only 50 centimetres long, is a treacherous predator. It exploits its shape to camouflage itself among the branches of the soft coral, blending into the background. When its prey approaches, the fish pounces.

36-37 This fish is named after its huge funnel-shaped mouth, which vaguely recalls a trumpet. It can suck its prey directly into its throat through its mouth. This operation only takes a fraction of a second, which means that it is hard to see, and almost impossible to photograph.

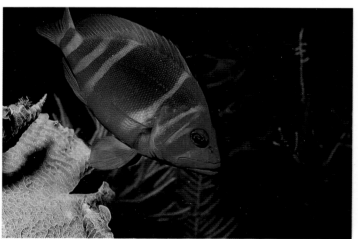

over from a vertical to a horizontal swimming position, and the strangely shaped goby. Cartilaginous fish hundreds of millions of years old, the predecessors of true fish with bones, also live here. Sharks and rays searching for food in the sand may also be encountered.

The southern stingray, which feeds on the animals it finds on the sea bed, is particularly famous. These fish can reach a wingspan of one and a half metres, and have a long tail with a venomous spine. However, despite common belief, the southern stingray is a perfectly harmless creature which only uses its deadly weapon to defend itself. On Grand Cayman Island they are actually included among the seven wonders of the sea. Hundreds of stingrays live in a place known as Stingray City, which has become a great attraction for divers and snorkellers.

At the point where the turquoise water turns to a darker blue, the ocean floor falls away steeply; this precipice is called a "drop-off" or "ledge". In this strip of ocean some of the larger inhabitants of the sea, such as the manta ray, eagle ray, grey shark, hammerhead shark and barracuda, together with large shoals of tuna fish and jacks, are to be found. Divers may also encounter the largest fish of all, the whale shark, over 10 metres long, which is also present in the Caribbean waters.

These waters, which are teeming with fish, provide the ideal habitat for dolphins too, and encounters with these intelligent mammals are common during boat trips along the coast or in the open sea.

They play in the ship's wake, entertaining passengers with their acrobatics. Great shoals of spotted dolphins, which seem to show no fear of man and will swim and dive with humans, live in some areas such as Bahamas Bank, north-east of the Bahamas. These waters do not only contain small cetaceans such as dolphins; every year between February and March, whole families of humpback whales swim past the Turks and Caicos Islands.

The beaches of the numerous islands and islets, where female turtles laboriously lay their eggs in the sand, constitute the ideal turtle hatchery. On moonlight nights it's fascinating to watch these reptiles emerge from the black waves like prehistoric monsters. Breathing heavily, they drag their heavy burden onto the shore to perform their task.

38 bottom left
The indigo hamlet (*Hypoplegtrus indigo*) is a timid creature which prefers to live among the corals near the surface of the reef.

38 bottom right
The rock beauty (*Holocanthus tricolor*) is another member of the angelfish family and is the smallest of the species.

38-39 The fairy basslet (*Gramma loreto*) is only 5 centimetres long. Half its body seems to have been dipped into a bucket of bright yellow paint. This fish may be encountered in the dark gorges at the base of walls and in grottoes, where it swims belly uppermost.

40 This image shows in detail a colony of painted tunicates which has taken up residence at the foot of a bright yellow tubesponge.

41 The tunicates are living creatures, no more than 2 centimetres long, which occupy a very high position in the scale of evolution.

42-43 The horse-eye jack *(Caranx latus)*, like the tuna fish and barracuda, is a predator fish which hunts in the open sea along the edge of the reef, and near its surface. Due to their great strength and streamlined structure they can reach very high speeds.

43 A shoal of horse-eye jacks *(Caranx latus)* swims up from the depths of the ocean towards the sun, creating silvery patches on the blue sea.

44 top Many fish, including the silverside, spend their lives in grottoes or wrecks, where they feel safer than in the open sea.

44 bottom The rainbow runner *(Elagatis bipinnulata)* usually swim in large shoals along the edge of the reef.

44-45 This picture shows a group of tarpons *(Megalops atlanticus)*, unmistakable thanks to their typical snout. Atlantic tarpons can reach the respectable length of two metres. They live in shoals, hidden in gorges or inaccessible parts of the reef. They are covered with scales which reflect the sunlight, producing thousands of shades.

46-47 The white grunt *(Haemulon plumieri)*, like all the other members of this family, lives in shoals. This shoal has divided because of the presence of the photographer, but the fish will soon join up again, as they feel safer in formation.

Every female turtle lays up to 150 eggs in
different nests over several nights. While
the mother returns to the sea, swimming
for hundreds of miles in the open waters,
the baby turtles develop in their shells.
The outside temperature determines the
hatching time and also the gender of the
animals.

After 40 or even 60 days the baby turtles
hatch simultaneously, with a synchronisation which has never been explained.

A mass of tiny creatures scuttle hastily
down to the water, dicing with death on
their journey, as hundreds of frigate-birds
are lying in wait for this easy prey, and
those that escape the birds are liable to
end up in the claws of shore crabs. Only
half the baby turtles reach the sea unharmed, and in the first few days of their
lives other dangers await them, such as
predatory fish. Only one turtle in 5000
reaches sexual maturity.

This great wastage is necessary to guaran-
tee the survival of the species.

However, the natural balance is now seriously endangered. Turtles are increasingly
exposed to new environmental risks, and
are ruthlessly hunted by man. Despite in-
ternational legislation protecting these
creatures, the world population declines
every year.

The shallow, sandy coasts of the west
Caribbean and the Gulf of Mexico are the
habitat of a singular species of animal, also
sadly threatened with extinction – the legendary manatee or sea cow.

These colossal animals breathe air, feed on
water plants and are quite harmless creatures with highly social behaviour.

Christopher Columbus referred to sea
cows, which he believed were mermaids,
describing them as "by no means as beautiful and alluring as those portrayed by
artists".

There is probably more gold and silver on the Caribbean sea bed than in any other ocean. Only half of the enormous treasures purloined by the European conquerors from the New World reached their destination. The caravels, which were hard to manoeuvre, often went down in hurricanes and storms, or ran aground on one of the numerous sandbanks or reefs. The captains of the period not only had to cope with environmental dangers, but also with attacks by pirates and corsairs with designs on their precious cargoes. Protected by the islands and hidden in the bays, they lay in wait for galleons on ships flying the skull and crossbones, and engaged in spectacular naval battles which they nearly always won. During these battles, numerous ships were set alight and went down with the loss of all hands as well as the cargo. With the aid of documents and writings of the period it is possible to trace the old navigation routes and reconstruct these events. As a result, entire fleets of ships with modern equipment patrol the seas in the hope of finding sunken treasure. Ballast, cannons, pieces of metal, gold, silver and precious stones are the only objects which have withstood the ravages of time. As the wrecks of these once proud ships are covered with sand and coral, the search is of-

ten a difficult task. In some cases, however, research, financial investment and tenacity have borne fruit, enabling treasures worth millions to be recovered. The Caribbean is a paradise for snorkellers and divers; this wonderful world represents a continual challenge to them. From the Florida Keys to the Lesser Antilles, a magical underwater landscape awaits the visitor.

On all the islands and along the coasts open to tourists there are well equipped diving bases which allow guests to visit the most attractive spots. The most famous diving areas in this western part of the Atlantic (from north to south) are the Florida Keys, the Bahamas, the Turks and Caicos Islands , the Mexican peninsula of Yucatan and Cozumel Island opposite, Cuba, the Cayman Islands, Belize, Honduras and the Bay Islands, the Virgin Islands, the French Antilles, and the Netherlands Antilles with Bonaire and Curaçao.

50 This large specimen of a black grouper *(Mycteroperca bonaci)* peers into the lens of the camera with a quizzical expression. The various species of grouper are voracious predators, which suck their prey into their huge maw and engulf it in a single mouthful. That is why these fish, unlike moray eels and barracudas, do not have sharp teeth.

51 Depending on their state of excitement and the activity in which they are engaged, groupers can change the intensity of their colour in just a few seconds. Here, the basic colour of the black grouper *(Mycteroperca bonaci)* has changed, showing the magnificent patterns of its scales to even greater advantage.

52 A specimen of the gold coney grouper *(Epinephelus fulvus)*. This species, which belongs to the *Serranidae* family, cannot be identified by its colour, which changes several times during the life of the fish: from brown to red, but even a two-tone colour body or spotted.

52-53 Perfectly camouflaged in its natural environment by the patterns of its scales, this black grouper *(Mycteroperca bonaci)* moves in and out of the coral. Nothing escapes its sharp eyes, and approaching prey is instantly captured and devoured.

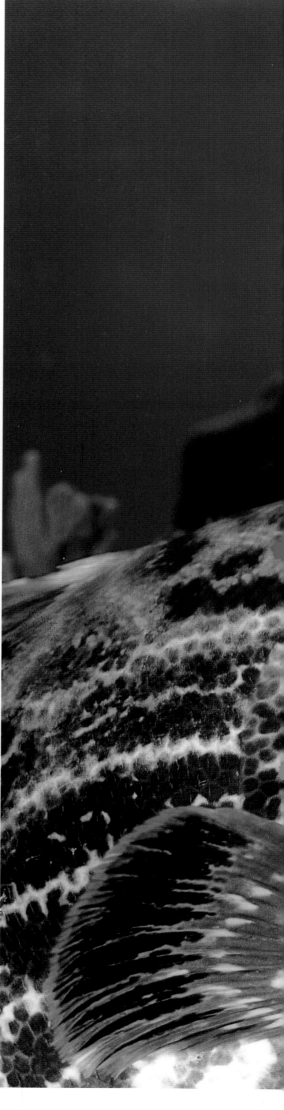

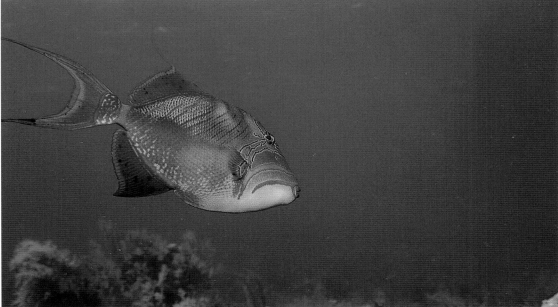

54-55 The name of the spotted trunkfish (*Lactophyrs bicaudalis*), certainly suits it! Despite its shape and small fins, this ungainly, ruthless fish is a fast, agile swimmer.

54 bottom These two fish belong to the same species. The image shows two specimens of the white spotted filefish (*Cantherhines macrocerus*), while they are performing their courting ritual before mating.

55 top The queen triggerfish (*Balistes vetula*) rarely approaches the lens. Although fish are curious by nature, they always keep at a safe distance.

55 bottom The horns above its eyes and the geometrical patterns on its body let the honeycomb cowfish (*Lactophrys polygonia*) be easily recognized.

56-57 As suggested by its huge eyes, the longspine squirrelfish (*Holocentrus rufus*) is a mainly nocturnal creature. During the day these fish stay near the reef, hiding in corners and crevices, or swim through underwater caves. At night they swim along the reef in search of food. These fish mainly feed on plankton.

58-59 A group of
schoolmaster snappers
(Lutjanus apodus) swims
in and out of the soft and
hard corals of the reef.
These blue fish, always
encountered in shoals,
live along the coral reef.

60 The coney grouper *(Cephalopholis fulva)* is the most attractive of the twelve species of grouper which populate the Caribbean: the splendid red background is studded with red spots with a darker edging. As in the case of all members of the grouper family, this pattern is a kind of camouflage, so that the fish blends in with its environment when lying in wait for its prey. Its true colours are highlighted by the flash.

60-61 The huge mouth of this grouper is awe-inspiring; this animal can swallow fish half as big as its own body. These fish usually live alone. During the mating period, however, hundreds of them gather in specific areas.

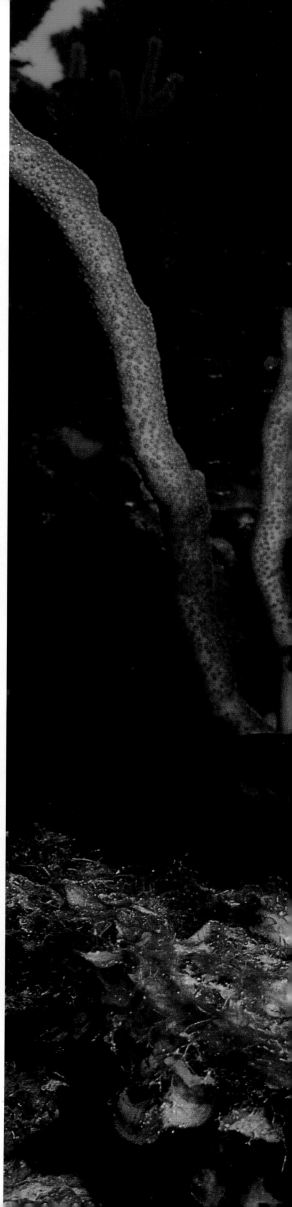

62 The nurse shark *(Ginglymostoma cirratum)* has, on average, a size which ranges between 1.5 and 2.5 metres. With a little luck, divers may encounter huge specimens, which can exceed 4 metres in length.

62-63 The nurse shark *(Ginglymostoma cirratum)* does not swim, and never hunts in the open sea. It procures its food on the sea bed, mainly eating prawns and molluscs. Unlike other sharks, which have to keep moving in order to breathe, this animal can supply its gills with oxygen by means of simple muscle movements.

64 Some fish capture their prey by pouncing on it, while others use an irritant poison. The scorpionfish is a camouflage wizard, as can be noticed in the image, and the unsuspecting victims swim straight into its huge maw.

65 The large-eye
toadfish *(Batrachoides
gilberti)* is equally skilled
at the art of camouflage.
It lives in dark gorges,
and can only be
encountered at night.
These fish can only be
found along the
Caribbean coast of
Central America.

66 Turtles have lived in the oceans for over 200 million years. Their appearance and behaviour has remained practically unchanged since the Mesozoic age. This green turtle *(Chelonia mydas)* swims away from the photographer with energetic movements of its flippers. Turtles have a great deal of stamina, as demonstrated by the fact that turtles tagged in the Caribbean have been found in the Mediterranean.

67 The hawksbill turtle *(Eretmochelys imbricata)* is the most attractive of all the turtles. When it is not hidden by barnacles, its shell has a magnificent yellowish-brown colour. The hawksbill grows to a maximum length of 60-90 centimetres; it certainly cannot compete with the green turtle or the loggerhead *(Caretta caretta)*, which lives in the Caribbean and can reach a weight of 250 kilos.

68 The barracuda *(Sphyraena barracuda)* is present throughout the Caribbean, and is frequently encountered. Up to a certain age these fish live in shoals, after which they separate and venture alone into the underwater world.

68-69 Its aggressive appearance and curious behaviour have given the barracuda *(Sphyraena barracuda)* the reputation of being a very dangerous fish. Although they can grow up to 1.5 metres long, they are totally harmless; no attacks on human beings have ever been reported.

70 The setting sun creates a mysterious atmosphere in the underwater world. Rays of sunlight reflect on the bodies of the Atlantic spadefish *(Chaetodipterus faber)*, producing thousands of facets.

70-71 The shape of its body recalls the suit of spades on playing cards, after which this fish is named. Like many other species, even the Atlantic spadefish *(Chaetodipterus faber)* can change its colour. Divers may encounter a spadefish with dark stripes in the open sea, and just a few minutes later see it again under a coral rock, in all the splendour of its gold shades.

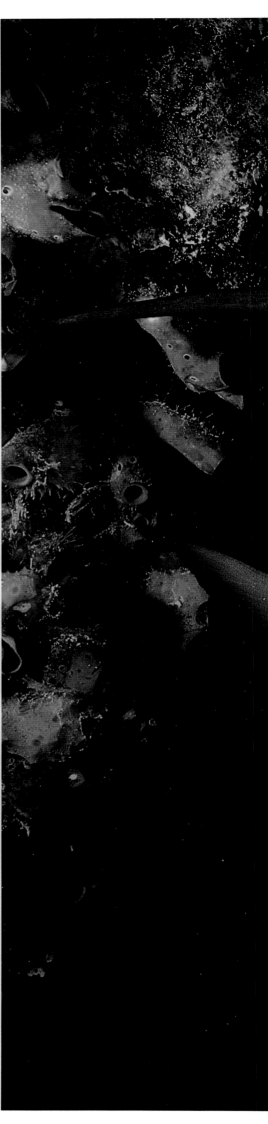

72-73 All friends together! In the midst of this shoal of bluestriped grunts *(Haemulon sciurus)* are some white grunts *(Haemulon plumieri)* with their silvery shades. The two species, which belong to the same family, have similar behaviour and feeding habits, and therefore accept one another.

Dolphins: Ambassadors of the Ocean

Luckily the forecast hurricane has passed by, moving south of the Bahamas in a westerly direction. However, the tail end of the hurricane has made the sea around the island very rough, preventing all underwater activity. Today is the first sunny day at Bahama Bank with no wind at all, and the water is flat calm. Suddenly, a breeze felt near the boat makes me jump. Great, my perseverance has paid off – the dolphins are back. The marine mammals which gather around our boat are not common dolphins, but Atlantic spotted dolphins (*Stenella frontalis*).

They usually arrive at Bahama Bank en masse at this time of year. During the storms of the past few days these intelligent animals took shelter in the open sea, waiting for the weather to improve. With flippers, mask and underwater camera equipment I slip overboard, my heart beating wildly with excitement. I've only come across untrained dolphins on a few occasions, and I secretly hope they'll let me come up close. Dolphins are cetaceans – mammals which live in all waters, including cold and warm seas and freshwater rivers. The family of dolphins is the most highly evolved, and includes over 30 different species.

74-75 The term cetaceans includes whales and dolphins. Twelve species of whale and twelve species of dolphin are represented in the Caribbean, most of which live in the open sea. With luck, divers may encounter two members of the dolphin family. This is a school of Atlantic spotted dolphins (*Stenella frontalis*).

Dolphins are long-lived marine mammals with a strong sense of family and highly social behaviour within the group, which generally consists of animals of different generations. They learn and grow up in the group and use numerous senses, especially sound, to communicate. As a result of their streamlined shape they can reach speeds of up to 60 kph, and their highly developed sonar system enables them to locate obstacles and their prey with astonishing precision.

The best known dolphin is the bottle-nosed dolphin *(Tursiops truncatus)*, the species best adapted for life in captivity which is easy to train; they are consequently used for films and questionable entertainments in amusement parks. A fantastic sight meets my eyes. The sea bed here at Bahama Bank is formed by white sand studded with small blocks of coral. For miles and miles the depth is between 10 and 15 metres.

A group of four dolphins is swimming in front of me with perfectly synchronised movements. The sun's rays slice through the water, reflecting on their muscular bodies. A female with her offspring, which does not yet have the characteristic spotted coat, has swum a few yards away, and seems to be scouring the sandy bottom in search of food.

They swim side by side; every so often the mother brushes against her baby and rests her head on his back. I wonder if this is a demonstration of motherly love, or if I'm watching a stage in the baby's education, which represents a key element in its relationship with its mother. Baby spotted dolphins live with their mothers until they are four and a half years old.

During these long years spent with their parents, the young dolphins obtain a wide variety of information and acquire a great deal of experience. It's amazing to see how complex their training is, and how much time the mothers devote to preparing their offspring to tackle all the situations they are likely to meet in life. Observation of dolphins has demonstrated that the fathers encourage their male offspring to engage in mock fights with their peers, or direct them towards other typically male activities.

The females are taught by their mothers at an early age to care for the young or assist in delivering babies. All this makes the younger generations aware of the existence of principles of responsibility and community life, which helps them mature. Within this structure there is also a complex communication system consisting of sounds,

76-77 A female dolphin with her offspring. All dolphins, including the Atlantic spotted dolphin *(Stenella frontalis)*, look after their young until the age of four. During the long years spent with their parents, the young dolphins collect numerous items of information and gain a great deal of experience. It's amazing to see how much time the mother devotes to training her young every day to tackle all the situations they are likely to meet in life. The fathers also have a specific role; they teach their offspring the rudiments of hunting and how to behave in a group.

movements and forms of contact. These elements and these forms of interrelation create the ideal environment for the young dolphins.

Why man is so interested in dolphins is a mystery. Is it their altruistic nature, their sense of responsibility and intelligence, or their gaiety and the smiling expression caused by the anatomy of the mouth? Since the time of Aristotle there have been stories of dolphins seeking contact with man, and these encounters are often documented. However, it would be wrong to believe that all dolphins become friendly with man. The clownish Flipper image with which dolphins have been labelled as a result of their questionable use in dolphinariums by no means reflects their usual behaviour. I keep following the female dolphin and her baby.

For several minutes they've been carefully searching at a specific point of the sea bed, where the mother stirs up a vortex of sand with her tail. My presence doesn't seem to bother them at all. Every so often, perhaps alerted by the sound of my camera shutter, they turn and stare at me. The company of these animals delights me, but this feeling alternates with mo-

ments of sadness. Tragically, man's love for dolphins has led to their being ill-treated all over the world. Baby dolphins are captured and used in shows held for purely commercial purposes. As a result, the happy family life they had been used to is rudely interrupted, and their social structure endangered.

It's like separating a three-year-old child from its parents for ever; the physical development of the dolphin is suddenly arrested, the separation from the group causes serious psychological harm.

This trauma, together with many other factors, is the reason for the great suffering and early death of dolphins living in captivity. Dolphins are intelligent creatures with a strong social sense, which is why they must live in groups and with their families.

They need to move freely in the immense reaches of the ocean to give vent to their energy. This is their world, and has been for millions of years.

78-79 Dolphins are cetacean, mammals which live in all waters, including freshwater rivers. Dolphins are long-lived, highly intelligent aquatic mammals with a strong sense of family and highly social behaviour. Due to their streamlined shape they can reach speeds exceeding 60 kph, and their highly developed sonar system enables them to locate obstacles and prey with exceptional precision.

80-81 The best-known dolphin is the bottlenose *(Tursiops truncatus)*, the species best suited to life in captivity. Sadly, they are used for questionable shows at marine parks and funfairs. It would be wrong to believe that dolphins make friends with man: they usually avoid contact with humans, although there are some exceptions. This untrained bottlenose dolphin lives on Lighthouse Reef, in Belize. It detects the presence of divers with its sonar system, swims up to them and accompanies them on their excursions.

ANGELS OF THE SEA

The beauty and elegance of the angelfish makes an encounter with them an unforgettable experience. Their name fits them perfectly; their large backward-trailing fins, resembling wings, enable them to glide gracefully along the coral reef. They can be identified from a distance by their bright colours and unusual shape. Divers who are lucky enough to come up close to them will be fascinated by the details of their fins, which recall filigree work, and the magnificent colours of their scales, which look like the work of an artist. Until a few years ago, marine biologists believed that these animals belonged to the great family of the butterflyfish. However, more detailed studies have revealed considerable differences. The angelfish family is now known by the name of *Pomacanthidae*, and is present all over the world. In the warm seas there are seventy-four known species of angelfish; their number is probably higher, but they have not yet all been catalogued. The largest numbers of angelfish are to be found in Australia, Papua New Guinea and Indonesia. Here in the Caribbean there are only seven species, but they are some of the most beautiful and majestic. From the Florida Keys down to Venezuela, from the Lesser Antilles to the

Bermuda Islands , divers and snorkellers encounter the angels of the deep on nearly all their excursions into this underwater paradise. Angelfish have a very unusual shape, which distinguishes them from other fish. Their body is very flat, or rather slender, and has a rounded profile. These fish, especially the queen, the French and the grey species, have a very attractive, pleasant appearance. They look like to have a small mouth with pronounced lips and a blunt snout. Angelfish are considered the queens of the coral reef by divers because of their exceptional beauty. Their long tail-fins undulate along the whole length of their bodies, giving them quite a streamlined shape. Their pectoral fins are paper-thin, with an elegant shape and pastel shades. The tail-fin is short and rounded, but perfectly suits the shape of the body. Those who think that fish have a stupid look will be surprised by angelfish. It's amazing how fast their pupils rotate in their sockets so that the fish can take in everything going on around it.

82 Angelfish have a special shape, which distinguishes them from the other inhabitants of the deep. Their body is very flat, or rather slender, and has a rounded profile. This photograph shows a grey angelfish *(Pomacanthus arcuatus)*.

83 A French angelfish *(Pomacanthus paru)* is silhouetted against the sea bed in all its splendour. Until a few years ago, biologists believed that angelfish belonged to the butterflyfish family. They are now known by the name of *Pomacanthidae*.

84-85 Angelfish are only active during the day. They usually swim in pairs, just above the reef, in search of food. The grey angelfish *(Pomacanthus arcuatus)* feeds mainly on soft corals, sponges, fish roe and seaweed. When night falls they hide in this maze of coral, safe from their voracious enemies.

86-87 Angelfish, in the image can be seen a specimen of French angelfish *(Pomacanthus paru)*, are considered the "stars" of the coral reef by divers, and rightly so, as their beauty is really exceptional. Their long tail-fins undulate along the whole length of their bodies, giving them an elegant shape.

An unusual feature is the fact that their eyes are set well forward. Experts believe that angelfish have binocular vision like man. I'm particularly fond of angelfish, and can't resist taking one photo after another. I admire their astuteness, and the mocking expression of their eyes when they make fun of me is quite unique. Angelfish are not shy by nature, and can sometimes be really curious. However, it is not easy to photograph these creatures, with their unparalleled elegance and beauty, as they keep disappearing into the reef. Taking up a diagonal position they dart into crevices and passages, and pop out at another point. Another interesting and unusual feature of angelfish is that they change colour several times in the course of their lives. From birth to adult age they change colour and pattern three times, so that an inexpert observer would never guess that it was the same fish. Angelfish are only active during the day. They usually swim in pairs, just above the reef, in a ceaseless search for food. Their diet is largely based on sponges, which offer no resistance to their small mouths. However, they also feed on tunicates, hydroids and sea fans. Divers may encounter these fish under the jutting coral rocks where the soft surface sponges grow. When night falls, they hide in the maze of coral, safe from their voracious enemies.

88-89 The images show three queen angelfish (*Holacanthus ciliaris*) swimming close to huge sponges. Sometimes these fish easily recognizable from the typical brilliant blue body and the gold-yellow tail, after meeting a diver, retreat a short distance but then turn to observe him a little bit closer.

90-91 The grey angelfish *(Pomacanthus arcuatus)* is one of the seven species representing the Pomacanthidae family in the warm waters of the Caribbean, from the Florida Keys to the coasts of Brazil and the West Indies, as far as the Bermuda Islands. It is easy to encounter this fish while swimming close to the reef, often in pairs, moreover it is relatively unafraid and let divers approach.

92-93 The Greeks called sea cows "sirens" which, in their mythology, indicated a figure half fish and half woman. This photo shows the typical behaviour of the West Indian manatee (*Trichechus manatus*). These animals present highly social behaviour, and live with their young in a family.

THE SIRENS OF CHRISTOPHER COLUMBUS

Dawn has not long broken, the water is flat calm, and only the reflections of the clouds in the overcast sky create a degree of contrast in this monochrome world. We've been on board our boat in the waters of Belize, off Manatee Creek, for two days. September is an understandably unpopular month on Mosquito Coast; the sun only rarely puts in an appearance, and it rains heavily at regular intervals. These problems do nothing to dampen our enthusiasm, however, because here, among the mangroves, live the legendary manatees, the last representatives of the *Sirenia*, a once common species of animal. We switched off the dilapidated outboard motor some time ago, and guide our dinghy along the creek with careful oar-strokes. I look around with great attention, listening carefully to the slightest noise in the hope of picking up a signal of their presence. I know for sure that these animals are close by, as they spend the night in deep holes among the mangroves. Two or three hours after sunrise they disappear into shallower waters, where they devour 40-50 kilos of water plants. Equipped only with flippers, mask and underwater camera, I slide carefully overboard. The water is murky; under the cloudy sky this underwater world presents no contrasts, and the diffused light creates an almost sinister atmosphere. I swim slowly to the centre of the hole where the sea bed falls away steeply. The visibility improves slightly, and suddenly the manatees appear before my eyes, huge and motionless on the sea bed. Sixty million years ago, strange four-footed herbivorous animals inhabited the earth. Over the millennia they adapted to the various environmental conditions, and three different species developed from these origins. Two of them – the elephants and the hyrax, a species now extinct – remained on land, while the third species, the manatees (*Trichechus manatus*, of the *Sirenia* family), took to the sea. The *Sirenia* are often called sea cows, probably because long ago great herds of these animals grazed on water plants. The Greeks called manatees sirens, a term which in Greek mythology referred to a being that was half fish and half woman. The first written observation about these animals was made by Christopher Columbus in 1493: "The mermaids we meet nearly every day have a face with human features, but they are by no means as beautiful and alluring as those portrayed by artists...".

Months spent at sea combined with the changing surface of the water may really have given the sailors the impression that

92 bottom left Most sea cows, now threatened with extinction, live in Florida, where special reserves have been created for them. However, they can also be found along the Caribbean coasts of Central America. They are not often encountered in the open sea, as they mainly live in the huge flat mangrove swamps along the Belize coast.

92 bottom right Adult manatees are shy creatures, which generally avoid contact with anything unfamiliar. Their young, however, are very playful, and may swim to within a few centimetres of a diver out of pure curiosity.

they had encountered the fabulous mermaids.

Manatees have a spine, and depending on the angle from which they are seen, can resemble a fat person. The body ends in a flat tail which, as a result of its horizontal position, acts as a powerful propeller. The animal is covered in thin hair, and does not have particularly good eyesight. Manatees grow up to 4 metres long, can exceed 500 kilos in weight, and live to be around 50 years old.

Unlike other animals, the males and females are the same size and the same colour. The face is covered by a short, bristly beard. The front paws or flippers are flat, like paddles, and careful observation reveals the presence of a kind of nails. This is certainly a prehistoric legacy of the time when their ancestors still lived on dry land. With their small ears, scarcely visible behind the eyes, the manatees can easily hear noises and their conversations, which do not consist of loud mooing but timid shrill sounds and whistles. These sounds are particularly useful in the murky water to ensure that the mothers and young do not lose one another.

The female manatee gives birth to a single offspring every 5 years, after a gestation period of around 13 months. As in the case of

dolphins and whales, the mother takes the newborn baby, weighing around 30 kilos, up to the surface to take its first breath. The dugs are located under the mother's pectoral fins. After a month the baby manatee can start to feed on small plants, although it will still be suckled by its mother for at least two more years. The mothers even lovingly suckle the offspring of other females, and live happily in communities. Manatees can live in both salt and fresh water. When they move with particular energy, they swim up to the surface to breathe every 2-4 minutes.

At rest they only need to breathe every 10-15 minutes, a facility which divers can only envy. When they are under water a kind of valve closes their nostrils, and the heart continues to pump at 30 beats a minute. As they are warm-blooded animals, manatees suffer the cold, and must live in water with a minimum temperature of 15°C. If they spend any length of time at a lower temperature they suffer from pneumonia and weight loss, as the animal is unable to eat and has digestive problems. As soon as the temperature falls they move south or seek the sources of warm rivers, as in Florida. They usually spend the months of January, February and March here, then split up and swim down to the coast.

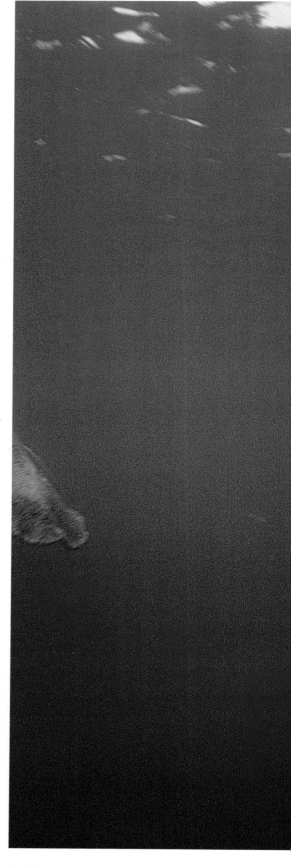

94-95 Manatees grow to a length of 4 metres, and can exceed 500 kilos in weight. Their diet is entirely vegetarian: an adult eats 40 to 50 kilos of water plants a day.

95 bottom left The front flippers are flat, like paddles, and have a kind of nails. This is certainly a throwback to the age when their ancestors still lived on dry land.

95 bottom right The only real enemy of these creatures is (and always has been) man. Although hunting of these animals has ceased, manatees are often killed by ships' propellers.

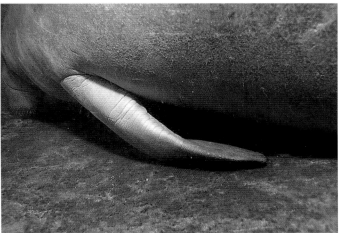

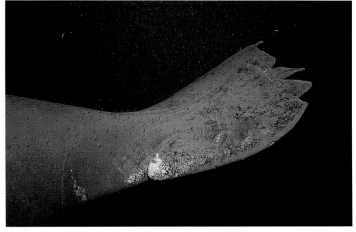

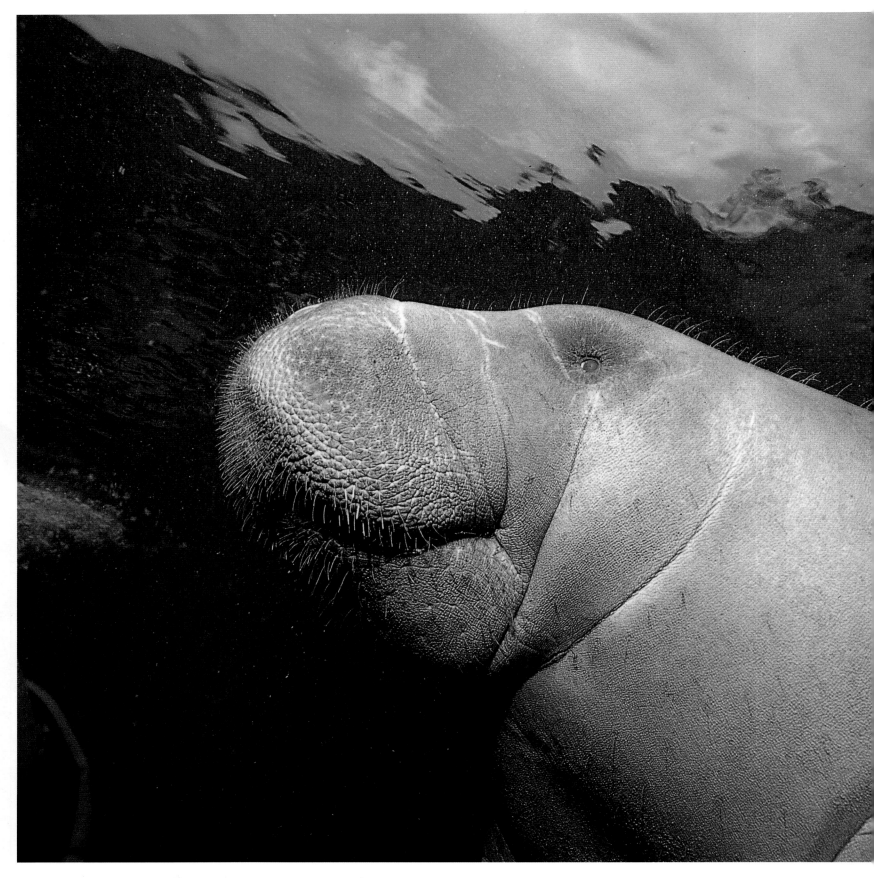

96-97 The ancestors of
the sea cow were curious
four-footed animals
which lived millions of
years ago. Of their
descendants, two species
(one of which is the
elephant) remained land
dwellers. Close
observation reveals the
similarities between
manatees and
pachyderms.

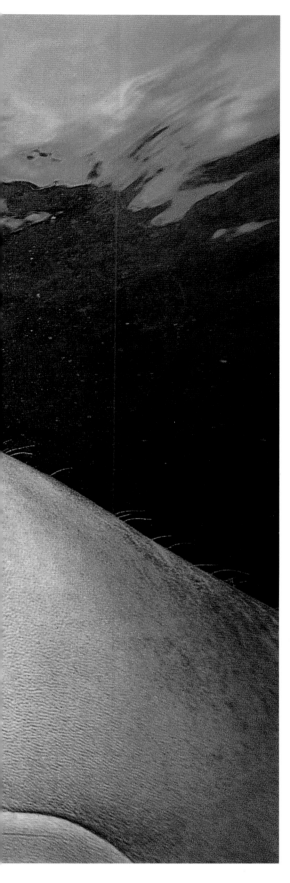

For centuries, manatees were hunted for their tasty meat, initially by the natives and later by the white colonists too. However, for a long time hunters have not been the worst enemy of these creatures. The causes of their imminent extinction are poisoning, temperature reduction, damming of rivers and above all, collisions with boats. The herds which were once numerous have been drastically reduced, and these mild, gentle creatures are forced to fight for survival. The northern manatee, called the Stellar Sea Cow, has long been extinct. In the 19th century it took Russian whalers and skin hunters just 27 years to exterminate this species, which had existed for millions of years. The West African manatee *(Trichechus senegalensis)*, the Amazon manatee *(Trichechus inunguis)* and the dugong of the Indian Ocean still exist. All three species are increasingly rare, however, and are seriously threatened. The living spaces of these creatures are systematically destroyed, and the sea cows are thus forced to abandon their once secluded, deserted territories for dangerous fishing grounds. Since 1983 the West Indian manatee has been protected along the eastern and western coasts of north America by very strict legislation. Only much later, perhaps too late, was it realised that much more needed to be done to prevent the extinction of these animals. In 1978 the Florida Manatee Sanctuary Act was passed, and the State of Florida was declared a manatee sanctuary. Other Caribbean countries have also protected these animals, in some cases by creating areas to which access is impossible. Along the coasts and rivers visited by manatees, boats can only move at walking pace. However, the authorities record an excessively high number of deaths among these animals every year which are not attributable to natural causes. And how many would there be if these protective measures were not taken? Manatees have adapted to their environment over millions of years, and scientists have also noticed an adaptation to the present situation. These animals have become shyer, move almost exclusively at night, and swim along the river banks where they will encounter fewer boats. However, time is fast running out. Can the manatee adapt fast enough to survive? The only real enemy of these creatures is (and always has been) man, and it is man who is now trying with all his might to help them. Man represents the only hope for the last of the mermaids.

98-99 The splendid
toadfish *(Sanopus
splendidus)* can only be
encountered when
darkness falls, near the
Mexican island of
Cozumel. This endemic
fish lives on the sea bed
or among the coral,
where it lies in wait for
its prey: invertebrates and
fish.

98 bottom A spotted
goatfish *(Pseudopeneus
maculatus)* in its
nocturnal livery. The
goatfish only display these
splendid colours, entirely
different from their
daytime colours, while
they are asleep.

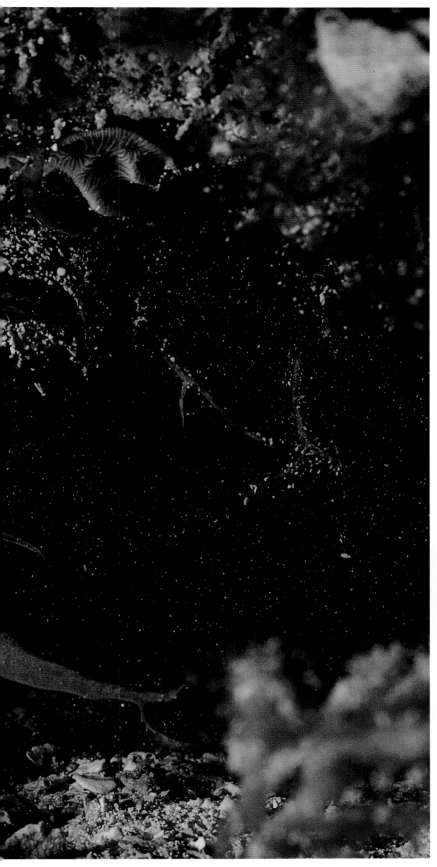

NIGHT IN THE REEF

The fiery sun sinks below the horizon. We're sitting on the quarter-deck of our boat, enjoying the peace and quiet. We dropped anchor on a huge sandbank in the lee of a long reef, and the slight current has brought the keel almost parallel to the coral reef. A slight breeze ruffles the surface of the water, and every so often breaks up the smooth surface. The transparent water enables us to identify every detail of the coral bed, as if I was looking in an aquarium. This is the time of day when sea creatures suddenly seem to

99 The porcupine fish *(Diodon hystrix)* has no need to fear larger fish. Like all species belonging to the puffer family it can swell up with water and turn into a rigid ball, bristling with spines, which cannot be devoured.

come alive; not much later, all goes quiet again, as rapidly as night falls in the tropics. I have often seen the sunset from underwater, and witnessed this fascinating spectacle. After a wild chase, great jacks gorge as if there were no tomorrow. Snappers, groupers and parrotfish hover with open mouths and extended fins in front of the "cleaning stations" where skilful prawns and grooming fish clean their teeth, gills and skin.

Many nocturnal predator fish have already left their hiding places and are hunting the tiny fish which swarm above the coral banks under the last rays of the sun like gnats around a light. Golden reflections dance under the surface of the water as sunbeams strike it.

It takes a little longer before the reef finally goes quiet again. Then, this underwater world shows its second face, which is completely different from its daytime appearance. Not until most fish have hidden away to sleep do the creatures of the night slowly appear. These weird yet graceful creatures feed almost solely on plankton, which increases in the darkness. For many of these animals this is their only chance of feeding, as appearing during the day would mean certain death. One example is the small coral-secreting polyp. Incredible as it may seem, these living creatures, which live in colonies of billions, are the architects of the reefs. The surface of the coral banks, apparently inanimate during the day, now comes to life as these tiny animals stretch their tentacles out of their refuge to capture plankton. It's a fascinating sight to see how these creatures, which are just a few centimetres or even only a few millimetres long, manage to procure food in the water

with their tentacles. With a synchronisation which has never been explained, their tentacles wave wildly in search of micro-organisms, which are taken to the mouth, located in the centre of the body. Night falls on the reef, and numerous unknown species of starfish suddenly appear. They glide over the sea fans or sponges to expose the largest possible area of their bodies to the water. A very unusual and attractive member of this species is the basket-starfish. Every attempt by divers to encounter them in the light of day will be frustrated, as they curl up and hide among the coral branches. At night they come out and show themselves in all their glory, a tangle of entwining snake-like arms. Starfish, sea urchins, crustaceans, sea anemones and turbellarians have been busy for some time now, whereas the shells and sea slugs take their time. It is long after sunset when divers find that the sandy sea bed has suddenly come alive, and numerous molluscs are making their way to the surface.

100 Moray eels go to sleep at sunrise. Morays are nocturnal creatures, which take advantage of the darkness to hunt their prey or lie in wait.

101 Morays relay solely on their acute sense of smell in their nocturnal hunting expeditions. The pronounced openings on the head of this goldentail moray *(Gymnothorax miliaris)* are clearly visible.

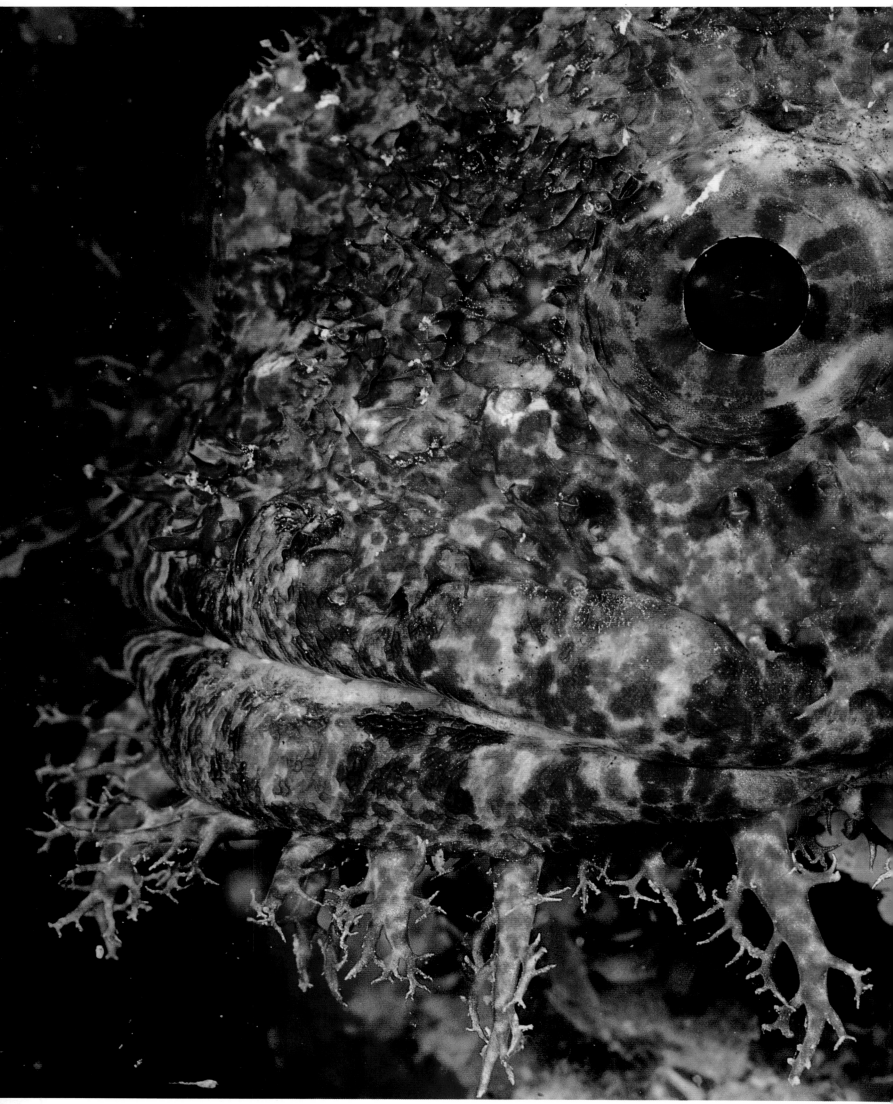

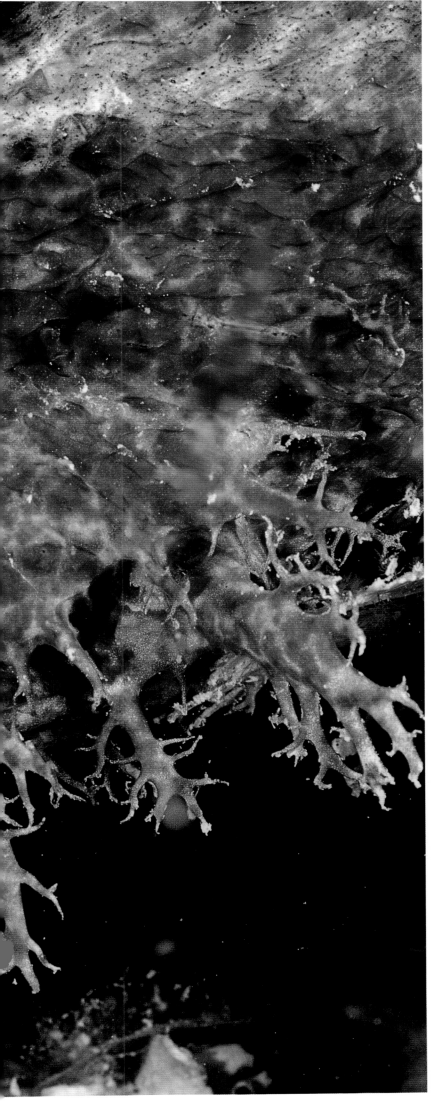

102-103 This bearded fish is none other than a large-eye toadfish *(Batrachoides gilberti)*. Its perfect camouflage makes it hard to spot. However, this fish can emit intense sounds, similar to a growl, which are audible under water from a distance of several metres.

103 top Although this scorpionish *(Scorpaena sp.)* is not a true nocturnal animal, it can only be encountered in grottoes or near walls. Like all the other members of its family it has spines on its back containing a dangerous poison.

103 bottom A yellow stingray *(Urolophus jamaicansis)* searching for food in the sand. This stingray, with its length of 35 centimetres, is the smallest of the family.

Sea slugs are large predatory creatures; they scour the ocean floor in search of food, and do not hesitate to devour members of their own species. Some slugs kill their victims with poison; for example, the conical sea slug launches poisoned darts that can kill fish in just a few seconds.

The poison in the cone can prove lethal even to man. These invertebrates procure their food quietly, usually without a battle or any particular fuss. However, tranquil as it may seem, night-time on the reef is by no means peaceful. Numerous predator fish take advantage of the darkness to attack their prey.

The reef is patrolled by barracuda and sharks, whose highly developed sense organs detect everything that goes on in the water. The snake-like moray eels glide over the sea bed, relying totally on their sense of smell. They have set their sights on some sleeping fish which, once captured, cannot escape their mouths, bristling with teeth. However, in order to pass the night undisturbed, many sea creatures take special precautions.

The parrotfish defends itself against its enemies by secreting mucus from the mouth, which wraps around the body like a cocoon.

This film does not protect it against bites, but prevents predators from sniffing it out. During night dives, divers are quite likely to come across cephalopods, a class of molluscs which includes the octopus and cuttlefish. Many people are not very fond of these legendary creatures, and the mere idea of encountering an octopus in the dark sea makes them shudder.

However, there's nothing to be worried about. Cephalopods are peaceful, shy creatures with great intelligence, which they exploit to capture their prey.

It's an unforgettable experience to follow the movements of an octopus on the sea bed. This animal continually changes the colour and structure of its skin and its shape.

Sometimes it glides flat and elongated along the sea bed, then pops up with inflated head and extended tentacles. Before attacking its prey it rears up in all its majesty, then pounces in a great leap. If it has to escape, it squirts out water from a kind of siphon, creating a backwash.

These animals can also produce a jet of black ink which makes them invisible as they escape.

104-105 Not all crustaceans have a protective shell. The hermit crab procures empty shells which it drags along with it to use as a home. The star-eye hermit (*Dardanus venosus*) is recognisable by its bright blue eyes.

105 This giant hermit (*Petrochirus diogenes*) will soon need to find a new home, as its present residence has got too small for its huge claws.

106-107 The social feather duster (*Sabellastarte magnifica*) has an easy life. Its body is contained in a kind of calcareous tube; to procure food, this worm simply stretches out its tentacles into the water to trap the micro-organisms carried by the current.

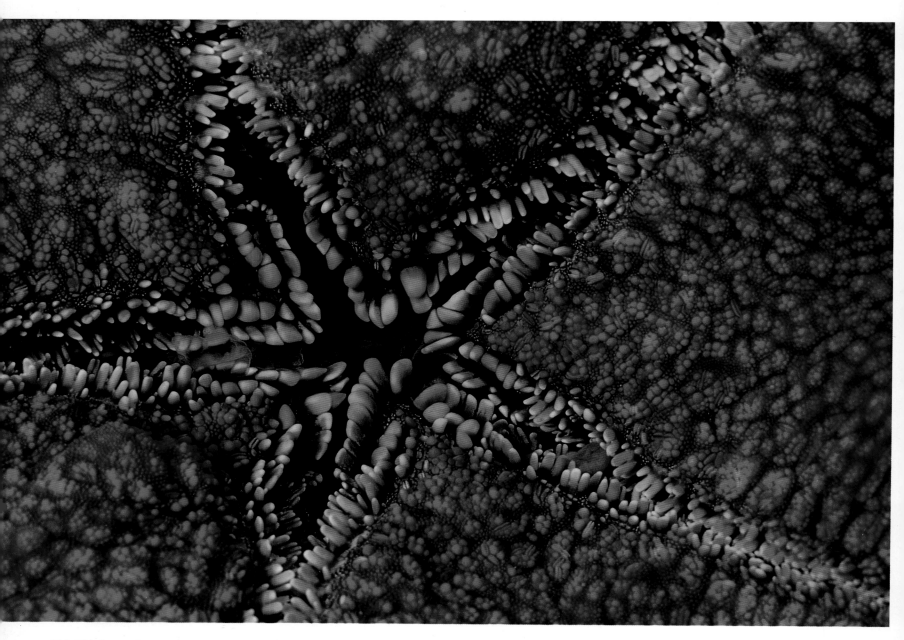

108 This image shows in detail the open mouth of a cushion sea star *(Oreaster reticulatus)*, which lives on the sandy sea bed and among the zostera. Starfish, which belong to the echinoderm family, are voracious predators.

109 This spotted cleaner shrimp *(Periclimenes yucatanicus)*, only 3 centimetres long, lives in symbiosis with sea anemones. Sea anemones paralyse other creatures with their stinging tentacles, and this shrimp is the only one which receives hospitality and comes out unharmed. A characteristic feature of the shrimp is that it rests on the tentacles of its host and uses its antennae to trap small fish, which are then devoured by the anemone.

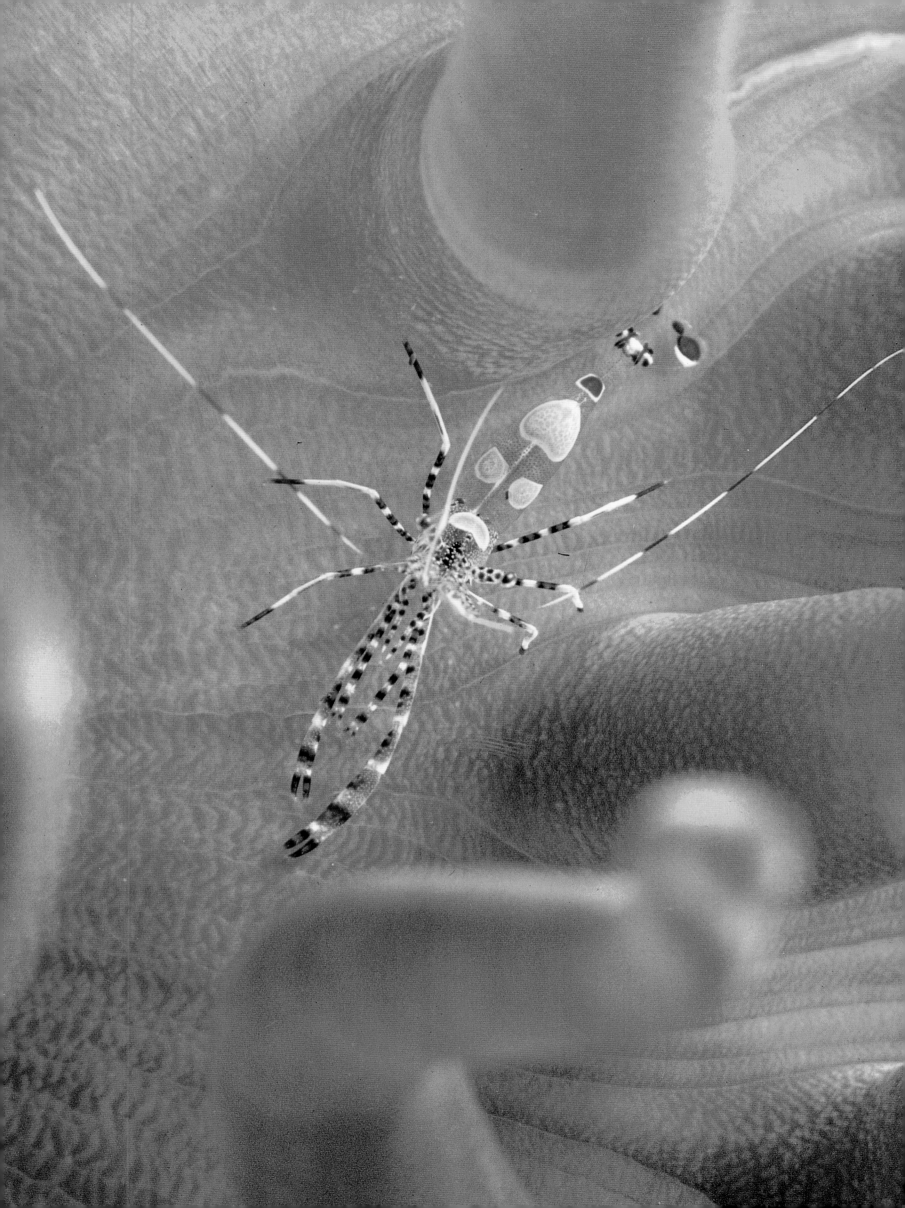

110 In this picture can
be clearly be observed
the strange *Stenorhynchus
seticornis,* a crab that
scuttles over the coral
banks on its long legs,
digging out anything
edible from the pores
and crevices with its
slender claws.

111 It's a real stroke of luck to encounter a decorator crab *(Podochela sp.)*. These crabs, only 5 centimetres long, are very good at camouflage. Amazingly enough, they cover their bodies with sponges, seaweed and hydroids, which continue to live happily in their new habitat.

112 Sponges, hydroids and a large colony of magnificent painted tunicates *(Clavelina picta)* cover a dry branch of black coral. The tunicates feed on micro-organisms: these living creatures, no more than 2-3 centimetres long, can pump water - from which they filter the necessary nourishment - through their bodies.

113 This rose lace coral *(Stylaster roseus)* grown on a branch of yellow fire coral *(Millepora alcicornis)* presents a fantastic play of contrasts. Fire coral stings unpleasantly and in the event of contact, the consequences are painful for man as well as other creatures.

114-115 The giant anemone *(Condylactis gigantea)* is the largest anemone in the Caribbean. Sea anemones belong to the Actiniaria family; they are carnivorous creatures, which paralyse their victims with their stinging tentacles. Most of them live in symbiosis with a shrimp or crab.

116 top At first sight, the eye of this sea slug recalls a cyclops. It is a specimen of the hawkwing conch (*Strombus raninus*).

116 bottom During the day, most sea slugs take refuge under the sand or hide in the coral. After sunset they crawl along the sea bed like prehistoric monsters. They mainly feed on seaweed, but also on living creatures which they track down, relying more on their sense of smell than their eyesight.

116-117 Thirty-five thousand species of sea slug inhabit the oceans of the world. Most of them have a shell which protects their soft body. This structure, built by the slug itself, is made of calcium carbonate, a secretion emitted through the outer tissues.

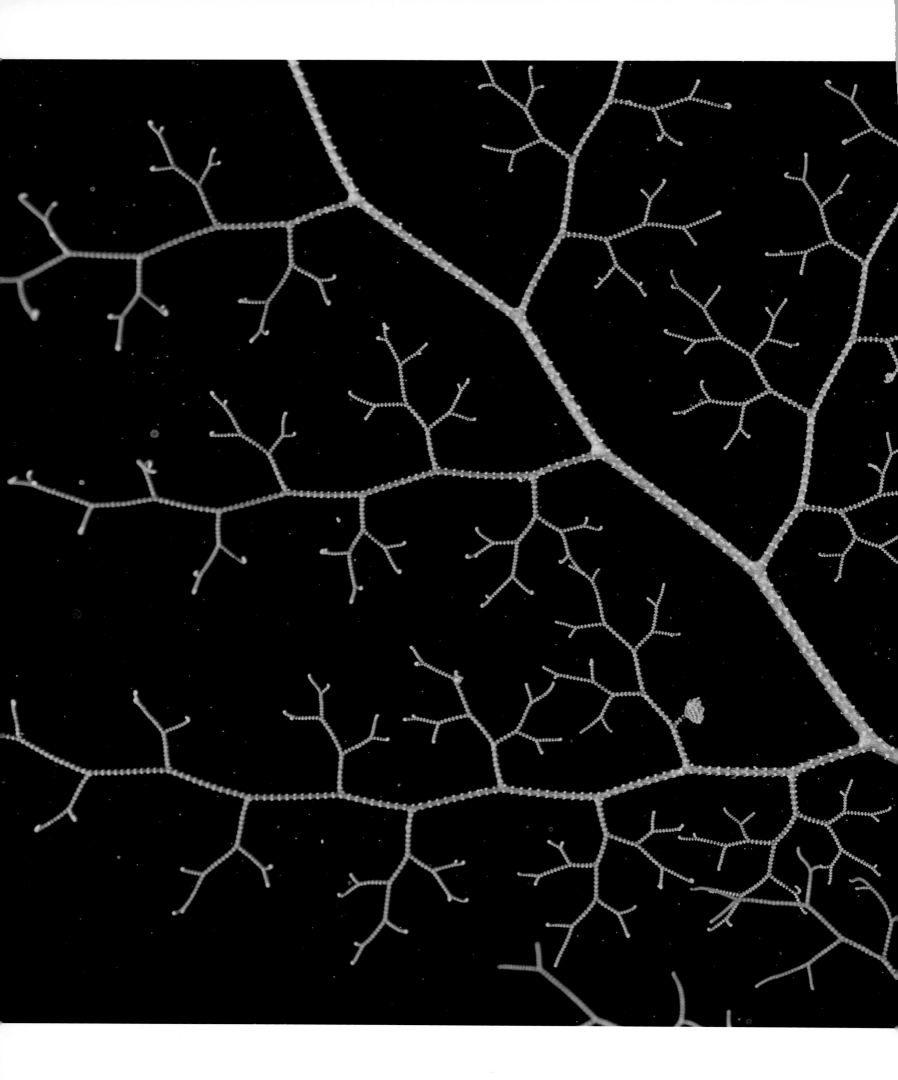

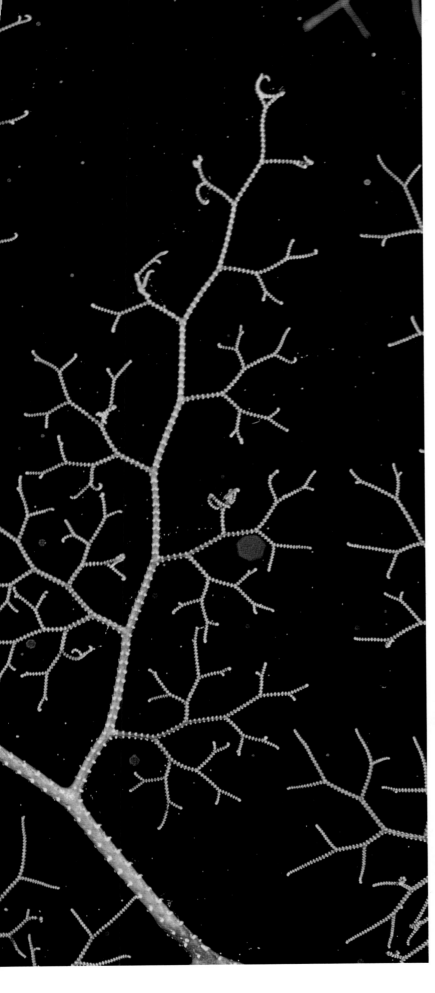

118-119 The giant basket star *(Astrophyton muricatum)* is a very unusual starfish. The filigree work shown in the photo is none other than the arm of a starfish in its juvenile phase.

119 Starfish are very sensitive to light. During the day they curl up and hide among the gorgonians and in crevices of the reef. At night they open on the coral banks or soft corals into the shape of huge fans, with a diameter of up to 60 centimetres. Starfish always face the opposite way to the current, which supplies their food.

120-121 The shell of the flamingo tongue *(Cyphoma gibbosum)* gleams like porcelain. As this slug hides its shell under its spotted mantle to camouflage itself, the shell is always clean. It lives on coral banks which it systematically scours at night in search of food.

121 This starfish, a sponge brittle star *(Ophiothrix suensonii)*, crawls over a sponge with unexpected agility. As they are hypersensitive to light, starfish always try to escape the beam cast by the diver's torch.

122-123 Macrophotography gives anyone the possibility to admire the delicate patterns and the brilliant colours that enlight the depths of the Caribbean Sea; this photo shows a red sea urchin.

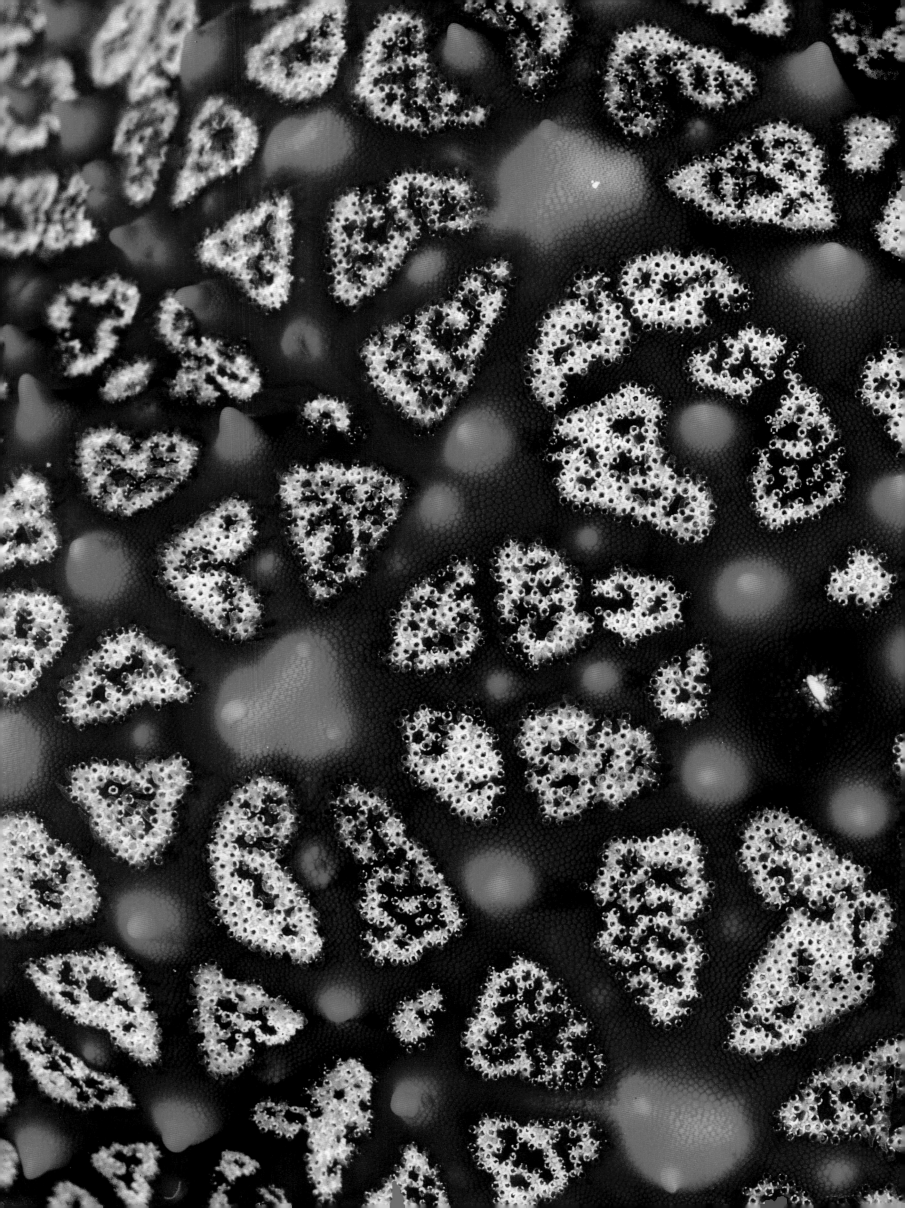

SPONGES: PLANTS OR ANIMALS?

124 top This huge yellow tube sponge *(Aplysina fistularis)* grows on overhanging coral walls.

124 bottom Sponges have very ancient origins; although their rigid body consists of actual cells, they have no muscles or nerves. This is a specimen of the branching vase sponge *(Callyspongia vaginalis)*.

If you observe the weird, immobile shapes of sponges, it will come as no surprise to find that they were classed as plants until the mid-19th century. Sponges have very ancient origins, and although their rigid body is made of cells, they have no muscles or nerves, and certainly no organs. The shape of the body is produced by a huge quantity of small calcium or silicic acid needles, and the cell mass is full of pores. The movement of the flagelli sucks water into the pores, where all the usable food particles are filtered. The water then exits through another opening. If sponges were plants, they should be able to produce a substance similar to that of the body from water with the aid of minerals, carbon dioxide and light. However, these cell elements have never been found in any sponge. Their choice of position is also significant; sponges do not depend on light at all, and grow in both light and shady spots. Sponges are mysterious yet fascinating creatures. For example, if a live sponge is passed through a sieve it will join together again. It is even possible to sieve two different sponges and obtain a single one which combines the cells of both. This regeneration is a unique event in the animal kingdom, and the result is that sponges come in all shapes and sizes. The most suitable habitat for sponges is water rich in food, with a slight current. The movement of the water constantly pushes new nourishment towards the pores of the animals. If the current were too strong, the union of the animals would be endangered, and if their pores were obstructed by substances carried by the water, they would face certain death. In the course of their evolution, which has lasted 600 million years, these creatures have adapted perfectly to new conditions. From the simple original siphons, various ramifications and cavities have developed, which act as a skeleton. The formation of cistern-shaped cavities lined with flagelli has enabled them to meet increasing supply and demand for food. Amazing as it may seem, the pore of a sponge, which has a diameter of only 0.08 mm, can filter 4.5 cc of water in 24 hours. A sponge grows to 30 cm in 7 years, and in the Caribbean, divers may encounter the giant orange sponges which grow to over 3 metres. It is not known how long sponges live; they probably die of old age when the layers of the body become too thin. The Caribbean offers the ideal habitat for sponges. Such a variety of species and such a large population is not to be found in any other ocean in the world. Wherever you dive in the Atlantic, you will find sponges. They can be encountered from 1 metre up to 300 metres down, where the weirdest living creatures dominate the deep.

125 The cell mass of sponges contains a multitude of pores, through which water is sucked and all usable food particles are filtered. The water then exits through another opening. This branching tube sponge *(Pseudoceratina crassa)* can grow up to a metre long.

126 and 127 No other ocean in the world contains as many sponges as the Caribbean Sea. In view of their weird shapes and the multitude of colours, it is not surprising that sponges were long classed as plants. If sponges were plants, however, they should be able to construct their own bodies from water with the aid of minerals, carbon dioxide and light. The fact that these cell elements have never been found in sponges proves that they are animals.

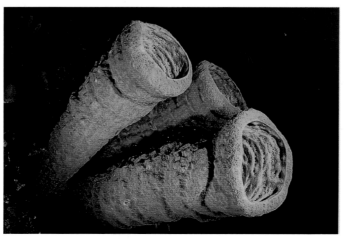

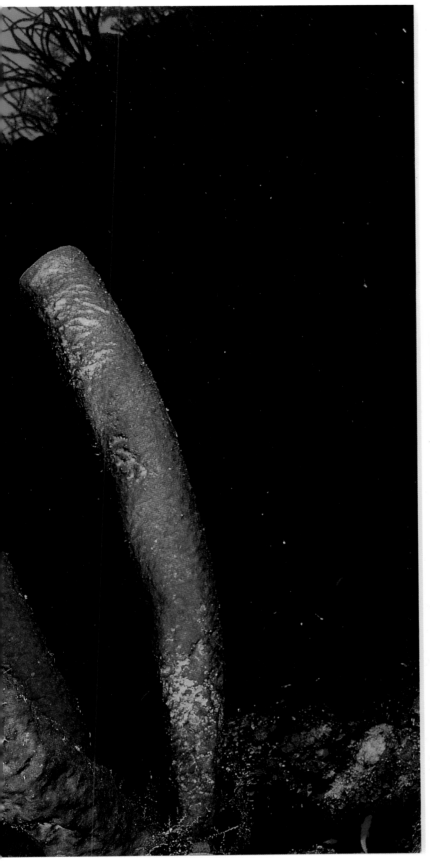

128-129 A characteristic feature of sponges is that even the most different cell colonies can live in close contact with one another. This photo shows a row pore robe sponge *(Aplysina cauliformis)* issuing from a huge yellow tube sponge *(Aplysina fistularis)*.

128 bottom Stove-pipe sponges *(Aplysina archeri)*, resembling huge trumpets, grow in the open sea.

129 Tubesponges rise vertically upwards from the surface of the coral reef.

130-131 No type of
coral or fish can boast
such a brilliant red as
these sponges. The erect
rope sponge
(Amphimedon compressa),
left, and the row pore
robe sponge *(Aplysina
cauliformis)*, right, live at
a depth of over 15
metres, in shady places,
especially near steep walls.

132 Nutrient-rich waters
stirred by a slight current
are particularly suitable
for the growth of
sponges. The presence of
these two elements offers
divers the chance to
encounter huge
tubesponges. Sponges
are also found in places
where the water is
dashed against the reef,
but in this case they only
grow to a modest size.

133 Quite by chance,
a fertilised sea anemone
cell has been deposited
on a sponge, and the
anemone has grown
among the siphons.
Two animals, considered
totally different since
their evolution, thus live
in perfect harmony.

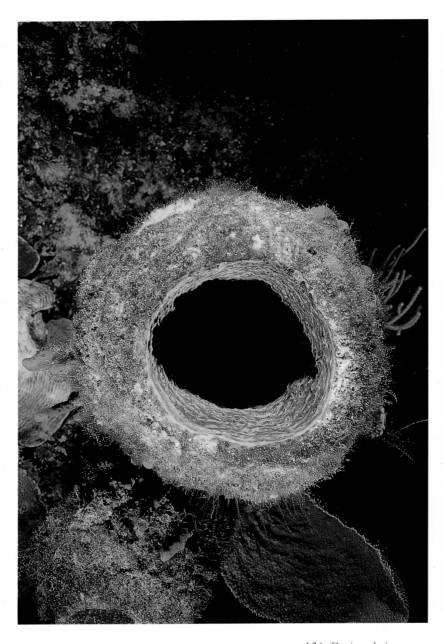

134 During their evolution, which has lasted 600 million years, sponges have adapted to new conditions. From the simple original siphons they have developed ramifications and cavities in order to increase their food intake.

135 The image shows a superb brown bowl sponge *(Cribrochalina vasculum)*. The perfectly modelled surface of this impressive sponge feels like sandpaper.

136-137 Grand Cayman
Island conceals a very
special secret. Stingray
City is a place on the
north coast of the island
where hundreds of
southern stingrays
(Dasyatis americana)
live.

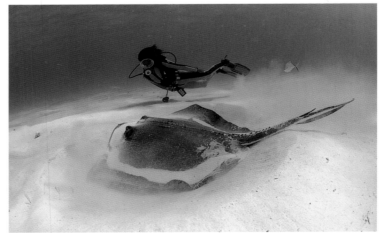

STINGRAY CITY

The Cayman Islands were discovered by chance by Christopher Columbus in 1503, during his fourth voyage to the New World. He disembarked on what is now called Little Cayman, which he named Las Tortugas because of the large number of turtles found there. The presence of these animals was also the reason for Spanish navigators' interest in the Cayman Islands, as they provided fresh meat. This exploitation of nature had unfortunate consequences; 40 years later the number of turtles had declined so sharply that the islands were of no further interest. On more recent nautical charts the islands were shown as Lagatargos, and in 1530 as Las Cayman, after the Indian term for small crocodiles. Sir Francis Drake, who stopped at Cayman after the sack of Santo Domingo, described it as a desert island populated by long snakes called *Caymanas*. When general peace was proclaimed in the West Indies in 1713, legalised piracy also disappeared. The last pirates, who included the famous Blackbeard, settled on Grand Cayman, so it comes as no surprise to discover that rumours of buried treasures abound there. Grand Cayman Island conceals other secrets, however. Apart from sunken wrecks, unexplored caves and coral walls which plunge to a depth of 1000 metres, there is a place along the northern coast of the island which has become famous with the name of

Stingray City. For generations, fishermen have dropped anchor in this spot, sheltered from the waves, to sort their catch. Numerous rays appear, and can be befriended by throwing them scraps of fish. In 1987 some divers, whose curiosity had been aroused by the tales told by the locals, went to take a look, and couldn't believe their eyes when they were surrounded by an enormous number of southern stingrays (*Dasyatis americana*) which manifested neither fear nor aggression. The news soon spread, and "Stingray City" became the main attraction of Grand Cayman. As the rays were fed by divers, this place soon became a veritable underwater zoo, and rules with a scientific basis were laid down to regulate visits to the area. The use of gloves is prohibited, and the fish can only be fed with sardines or cuttlefish. Before the bait is handed over to divers, they are taught to feed the rays correctly. This may seem excessive, but in fact it's by no means easy to feed a large stingray. As the mouth is at the rear of the body the animal is unable to see the tasty morsel, only smell it. The diver therefore has to position the bait under the ray's nose with closed fist and wait for the right moment to release it.

136 bottom The stingray can reach the respectable length of 2 metres. The tail, with its venomous spine, has given this creature an undeservedly frightening reputation. However, stingrays are wholly innocuous animals, which only use their dangerous weapon to defend themselves.

137 Rays are cartilaginous fish which, like sharks, have no bones. They are some of the most distant relations of the vertebrates, and their appearance has remained almost unchanged for millions of years.

138-139 Stingrays feed on shellfish, crabs and small creatures which they dig out of the sandy sea bed. The large spiracles above their eyes enable them to breathe when they are on the sea bed, hidden or camouflaged under the sand.

140 top and 140-141
The rounded shape of
the ray, with its slightly
raised profile, is well
suited to life on the sea
bed. The mouth, with its
strong jaw and flat teeth,
enables the ray to crush
the hard shells of
prawns, one of its
favourite foods, without
difficulty.

Many adult stingrays can be very intrusive, and
like to push divers into the sand with all their
weight and strength. There's no need to be
afraid of the venomous spine on the tail; not one
of the thousands of visitors has ever been injured.
In this lagoon, which is no more than 3 metres
deep, the weather is usually calm and transparent. The lagoon bed is flat, and dark spots indi-
cate the presence of coral banks which break up
the monotony of the white sand. There's no
need to go looking for the stingrays, which
already fire the visitor's imagination during the
boat trip; as soon as you dive into the water
they'll swim up in formation. There are rays of
all sizes, from the huge dark-coloured adults to
the paler young. They surround the divers like
great birds, and it doesn't take them long to
find out who has the bag of food. What hap-
pens next could be described as the "ray
dance", and provides a unique opportunity for
photography and video enthusiasts. Marine
biologists have obviously conducted research to
ensure that the large number of visitors and
constant feeding of the animals does them no
harm. But it doesn't; quite the contrary. Every
year the number of stingrays increases, and the
presence of numerous males and young has
been recorded recently. It's hard to estimate the
exact number of stingrays that populate Stingray
City, but there must be hundreds of them.

140 bottom The photo
shows the sharp,
venomous spine of the
stingray. It is located in
the initial section of the
long, whiplash tail,
inserted in a kind of
groove. If the ray needs
to defend itself, it lifts its
tail and whips it violently
around its prey. The bad
reputation of this creature
is undeserved; in fact, no
notice has been repoted
of divers that have ever
been stung by a ray.

142-143 The inhabitants of Stingray City do not know what fear is. As soon as their sensitive sense organs detect the sound of air bubbles from the diver's equipment, they swim rapidly up to him in a group.

THE WRECK OF SAINT-PIERRE

Radio message from Capt. Edward Freeman, captain of the *Rodam*: "We have just returned from the gates of hell! Telegraph worldwide the news that Saint-Pierre, capital of Martinique, has been razed to the ground with all its inhabitants!!!" It is 24th April 1902 and in the bay of Saint-Pierre at the foot of the Montagne Pelée, a large fleet was anchored. The island of Martinique was declared a French colony in 1835.

After the extermination of the native Arawaks and Caribs, slaves were imported from West Africa to work in the plantations. Martinique, like the neighbouring French islands, was already a major exporter of fruit, spices and sugar cane to Europe. At the port, on the quay and in the warehouses, hundreds of dark-skinned men were loading bottles of rum.

The dockers were mainly of Indian descent. From 1848, when the French governor Schölcher abolished slavery, they were imported from India as cheap labour.

Suddenly, a loud rumbling noise was heard, and all eyes turned to the Montagne Pelée, where a thin plume of smoke was rising from the summit of the mountain into the sky. Many immediately recalled the rumours of the past few days; workers on the farms

scattered along the mountainside had told of a tremor which made the earth shake, and a strange smell of sulphur in the air. They had also observed that the birds and other animals in the area instantly fled. Official sources announced that the telephone line connecting Martinique to the neighbouring island of Guadeloupe had been mysteriously interrupted.

25th April 1902: it is 10 a.m. Suddenly, a series of underground explosions similar to drum rolls was heard. Every two minutes or so the mountain spat out ash and smoke.

26th and 27th April 1902: the mountain was quiet. A plume of yellow smoke, blown south-west by the wind, was all that could be seen.

The fear which had spread among the population disappeared, and those who had fled the town returned to their homes.

28th April 1902: around midday, numerous small explosions were again heard, and the famous mushroom cloud rose from the summit of the mountain.

144 The new city of Saint-Pierre in the morning sun. Unusually, the peak of the Montagne Pelée is not shrouded in clouds. The volcano no longer represents a danger nowadays; not because it is inactive, but because an observation station fitted with the latest equipment records even the slightest variation.

145 The *Tamaya* was one of numerous ships which caught fire and sank in Saint-Pierre bay when the volcano erupted. The existence of this ship was unknown until a few years ago. The wreck of this majestic three-master now lies at a depth of 85 metres, intact and in the same condition as when it went down with all its crew a century ago.

146-147 Ellery Scott,
the captain of this vessel,
was one of the few
survivors of the disaster.
The vivid descriptions of
the event are his. His
ship, the *Roraima*, now
lies in Saint-Pierre bay at
a depth of 50 metres.

The nearby Rivière Blanche suddenly began to carry a huge and dangerous amount of water downhill.

29th and 30th April 1902: these two days passed fairly quietly, except for a few tremors which shook the town. The inhabitants of Saint-Pierre were visibly nervous, however, and uncertainty, fear and a feeling of helplessness were widespread.

1st May 1902: after a quiet night, a huge amount of ash issued from the mountain, accompanied by thunder and flashes of flame. The same phenomenon was repeated on the next two days. The entire town was covered by a thin film of ash. The population was panic-stricken, but the authorities exhorted the people to keep calm, assuring them that there was no danger.

4th and 5th May 1902: overnight the river became increasingly swollen, and the Montagne Pelée continued to belch out ash and smoke. The mountain claimed its first victims, when 25 workers from a rum distillery on the mountainside were engulfed by an avalanche of mud and clay.

6th May 1902: violent detonations shook the sleeping town in rapid succession.

Many panic-stricken inhabitants abandoned their homes. In the afternoon, Governor Mouttet travelled to Saint-Pierre with his wife and children to demonstrate that there was no danger.

7th May 1902: forty ships were anchored in Saint-Pierre bay. Understandably, fear and uncertainty spread among their crews. However, the port laws prohibited ships from raising anchor before they had loaded or unloaded their cargoes. In addition, many captains were too proud to be the first to start up the steam engines or hoist the sails and leave this sinister place as quickly as possible. Only one, Captain Ferrera of the steamship *Orsolina*, flying the Italian flag, did not hesitate to raise anchor. He had seen the eruption of Vesuvius in Naples, and had a terrible premonition. In vain he warned the authorities, and tried to get permission for all the ships to leave. Permission was refused, and heavy penalties were threatened. "There's nothing you can do to me – you'll all be dead tomorrow", was his reply. On the evening of 7th May the captain took his ship and his entire crew to safety.

8th May 1902: early in the morning Captain Ellery Scott, on board the steamship *Roraima*, scanned the land which lay just 200 yards away. It had rained non-stop all night, and now that the ash had been washed away, the town faced the dawn calmly. A new ship, the *Rodam*, had just arrived, and was moored at the customs house wharf. After the menacing events of the past few days, this seemed like the start of a new life. Scott gazed at the Montagne Pelée; only a small column of smoke was rising from the mountain peak.

147 bottom left Nature
has brought new life to
the *Roraima*: soft corals
and sponges have settled
on the superstructures.

147 bottom right The
upward-facing bow of the
Roraima. The hull,
encrusted with coral, is
entirely made of metal,
and will undoubtedly
survive on the sea bed for
another century yet.

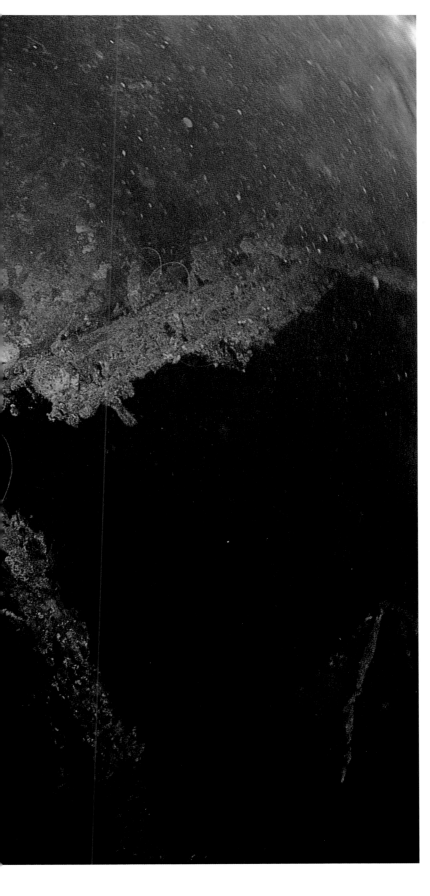

It was two minutes to eight. Captain Ellery Scott was never able to forget what happened next. With explosions and rumbling noises the mountain practically split in half. Ash, mud and flaming gas issued from the huge crater that had opened up. As soon as this cloud reached Saint-Pierre, darkness fell. Within two minutes the town and its 30,500 inhabitants were covered with white-hot ash. A man imprisoned in the old fortress screamed out in fear. Auguste Ciparis, who had been arrested for drunkenness the previous day, was the only inhabitant of Saint-Pierre to survive. As a result of the incandescent ash, all the ships in the bay caught fire. In the darkness caused by the ash and smoke, total chaos reigned. Nearly all the sailors died. Some escaped death by clinging to the remains of the drifting ships. They included Captain Ellery Scott, who provided this description. The *Rodam*, which had only just come into the bay, was saved by the fact that its engines were still running and that Captain Freeman kept a cool head; it reached the open sea, and the fire which had broken out on board was extinguished. All the other ships, including the *Roraima*, the *Dahlia*, the *Diamant*, the *Teresa Lovico*, the *Raisinier* and the impressive three-master *Tamaya* sank in the troubled waters off Saint-Pierre, which by now had been totally destroyed.

148-149 A diver has reached the interior of the wreck. The holds of the 100 metre long merchant vessel are totally burnt out. Large sponges now live on the iron structures and bracing, their bright colours gleaming in the light of electric torches and flashlamps.

148 bottom A steep companionway leads to the engine room of the *Roraima*. It's rather risky to venture inside the wreck, as sediment can obstruct the vision and make it difficult to find the way back.

150-151 Ships which sink in warm seas turn into artificial coral reefs in just a few years. As most of these wrecks lie on large beds of sand, they form veritable oases. Visits to wrecks are always fascinating, as they give a glimpse of the past and also shelter numerous life forms.

151 The steam boilers of the *Roraima*, which burst and were torn out of their housings following the explosion on board.

The photographs clearly show how corals, barnacles and other organisms have covered the metal plates over the years.

After 88 years and 7 months from the terrible cataclysm in front of us, under the morning sun, is New Saint-Pierre. The summit of the Montagne Pelée is enveloped in clouds. The volcano no longer represents a threat; not because it's inactive, but simply because an observation station with the latest equipment which records the slightest variation has been installed. In the past 6 days we have explored and systematically photographed all the wrecks in the bay. We've been lucky, as the usually murky water of Saint-Pierre was incredibly clear. These dives have given us an insight into the history of the disaster of Saint-Pierre. Today's a special day. Beneath us, at a depth of 85 metres, is the wreck of the *Tamaya*. The existence of this ship was unknown until 8 years ago, when a ship of the French navy which was preparing nautical charts located the wreck with sonar and marked it with a buoy. Jacky Imbert, one of the three divers who first explored the Tamaya, is going with me on today's dives. It was also he who, after numerous dives with Michel Metery, identified the ship's bell which revealed its identity: "Tamaya Liverpool 1862". Only a few divers have so far had the chance of seeing the *Tamaya*. Cousteau filmed the wreck from a submarine, but no-one has ever photographed it. It's a challenge, and also the fulfilment of a dream I've nurtured since I visited Martinique for the first time years ago. Since the depth-finder detected the indistinct profile of the wreck I've been strangely agitated, and for the hundredth time I've mentally gone over the various stages of the dive. In order to work at this depth you have to plan every detail; from the moment we dive in we have only 10 minutes before returning to the surface. I haven't the slightest idea what the light conditions will be like down there. "Allez-y!" I dive off the side of the boat equipped with a camera, and swim towards the slender yellow cable of the buoy which serves simply as a visual reference. 5 metres down we stop for a last check before continuing to the bottom; we check for leaks from the breathing apparatus, belt fastening, time, oxygen tank pressure, light, flashes and camera check. All OK.

152 The bow of the *Tamaya* is entirely covered with whip coral and sponges. The wreck lies deep down at a considerable distance from the point where the ocean floor falls away, which means that diving here is quite safe. Only a few divers have been lucky enough to see it for themselves. Filming this mysterious ship was one of the most exciting challenges of my life.

153 We remained at this depth for a very short time; the enormous water pressure and high oxygen consumption only allowed us to stay down for 10 minutes. A number of dives are needed to explore the wreck in detail. However, the conditions are not always right for diving: the currents and poor visibility sometimes play havoc with divers' plans.

154-155 The diver's torches project ghostly shadows and reflections onto the remains of the *Tamaya*. Although the superstructures were destroyed by the fire which broke out before the ship sank, and the length of time it has spent on the sea bed has severely damaged the non-metallic parts, the wreck is in an excellent state of preservation.

We can go on down to the abyss. I can't wait to see the wreck. My eyes search the monotonous dark blue water, with its diffused light, until they start to ache. Nothing. 60 metres – still nothing. 70 metres – there it is! The indistinct contour of the *Tamaya* stands out against the sandy sea bed. Slowly my eyes get used to the twilight, and I enjoy the view from above for a few seconds. The 60-metre 3-master is lying on her starboard side, her masts partly buried in the sand. She's in good condition for her age, and has hardly changed since she sank many years ago and was entombed here with all her crew. It's a unique sight. The plumbline of our buoy is right in the middle of the ship, so we can swim towards the bow as planned. 7

minutes left. We can start. I have Jacky in my view-finder; as agreed, he swims along the mast towards the hull. The beam of his electric torch projects spectral shadows onto the sandy ocean floor. I'm concentrating hard on the job in hand. The flash rends the twilight as I take one photo after another. My companion swims slowly along the port side, which is covered with great sponges and whiplash coral, towards the bow. From my position a fantastic view appears. Another 5 minutes left. We're on the bow; the bowsprit is lying in the sand.

155 bottom The torch light clearly reveals the ship's spare bow anchor. This anchor is thought to have been torn away from its original position on deck when the ship sank. It is now inside the wreck, hanging from a frame.

156-157 The great Blue
Hole of Belize, which lies
at the centre of Lighthouse
Reef, is one of the seven
wonders of the sea. It has
a diameter of some 400
metres and a depth of
145 metres. These blue
holes were formed
millions of years ago,
when the water level was
several hundred metres
lower than it is now.

156 bottom Diving into
the waters of the Blue
Hole is like going back
into the past: a truly
indescribable adventure
for the diver.

Blue hole: a dive into the stoneage

The single-engined Piper took off into the blue sky just a few minutes ago. We're flying over Mosquito Coast, as the coast of Belize is nicknamed, and heading out towards the open sea. Belize is famous for its coral reef, which runs along the whole length of the coast. It's 300 kilometres long, which makes it the second longest in the world after Australia's Great Barrier Reef. The great coral belt which almost reaches the surface of the water looks like a thin line in the ocean. We fly back and forth over this marvel of nature to take some photos of it. A magnificent spectacle appears. As if hurled by a gigantic hand, great banks of coral shine through the shallow turquoise water on the leeward side. They become thicker and thicker, until they blend into a compact wall which almost reaches the surface. The windward side falls away steeply, with a tail of pale blue water. Our destination is Lighthouse Reef, situated 75 miles from the coast in the open sea. This coral reef, which is 45 kilometres long and continues down to a depth of 1000 metres below sea level, is one of the most popular diving paradises in the Caribbean. Because of its position in the open sea there is a huge variety of fish, and there is a greater variety of coral vegetation than anywhere else because of the currents. However, the real attraction here is the great Blue Hole, one of the seven wonders of the sea. These blue holes are numerous in the Caribbean; for example, they can be found at Andros and Grand Bahama Island. The largest and deepest, however, is here, at the centre of Lighthouse Reef. These karst caverns were formed during the ice ages. At that time the sea level was several hundred metres lower, and huge amounts of water eroded the sandstone rocks. The presence of stalactites and stalagmites demonstrates that these caves were once dry. Later, when the entire area was covered with water, the ceiling collapsed, leaving this typical round sink-hole. In 1972 the great oceanographer Jacques Cousteau discovered the secret. In a daring venture he took the *Calypso* into the Blue Hole and explored it as far as the ocean floor in mini-submarines. The Blue Hole of Belize has a diameter of approximately 400 metres and a depth of 145 metres. The walls all round are perpendicular: huge stalactites, some over 5 metres long, hang from the overhangs 40 metres below the ceiling. The Blue Hole is not inhabited by animals and plants of any particular interest, but that does not make a visit to it any less fascinating. Diving in these dark waters is like going back in time – a truly indescribable experience. The Blue Hole, with its dark blue colour and perfectly circular shape, is right under us.

158 Huge stalactites hang from the ceiling, demonstrating that these caves were once dry. The twilight of the abyss produces an extraordinary spectacle.

159 Man looks small and insignificant by comparison with stalactites. Just think how long it took for incessant dripping to create this phenomenon; stalactites and stalagmites are produced by drops of water filtering through the rocks, which leave a calcareous residue as they fall.

Flying in large circles the pilot comes down lower and lower. This is the first time I've seen this wonder of nature from above, and my last descent into the Blue Hole comes to mind. We wanted to explore the north-west side of the Blue Hole, not far from the north entrance. Some American divers had told us that there were some especially attractive stalactites there. Our descent into the abyss began at the edge, where the ocean floor falls away in an almost perpendicular drop. We calibrated our equipment with particular care, and finally found ourselves swimming over a chasm 150 metres deep. Although the sun was shining brightly above us, it was already pitch black only 30 metres down. 40 metres! A black line marked the overhang under which the stalactites were to be found. The tension increased as we swam into the darkness. We were in the right place. Under the beam of light cast by our electric torches, which created a spectral landscape, our attention was caught by great cone-shaped outlines hanging from the ceiling; some had odd spiral shapes, while others featured odd protuberances and contours. It was an incredible sight! This adventure has remained indelibly impressed on my memory. Time flies down there, and we soon had to return to the surface. Slowly we swam towards the light, aware that we had spent a few minutes in the Ice Age.

160 The scales of the queen angelfish (Holacanthus ciliaris) have such magnificent colours that they almost look like the work of an artist.